FROM SARRIA TO SANTIAGO

A 10-Day Camino With Family and Friends

John Peters II

ISBN 978-1-7328984-5-5 (paperback)
ISBN 978-1-7328984-4-8 (e-book)

Library of Congress Control Number: 2023923600

Cover design by: John Louis Peters II
Printed in South Pasadena, CA, United States of America

Dedicated to Rosemary, Adam, and the Davidson family for making my pilgrimage an experience I will never forget.

CONTENTS

INTRODUCTION

In 2019, my wife Rosemary said she dreamed of walking the Camino de Santiago in Spain. As a Catholic, she felt the pilgrimage was something she should do. For me, it sounded like a fun adventure, walking 800 km across northern Spain for six weeks, meeting fellow travelers, staying at different places every night, and eating great food.

"When should we go?" I asked.

"When we retire in 10 years."

Thinking about my current aches and pains, I said, "We need to go as soon as possible. Who knows what can happen within the next ten years."

"I can't take six weeks off of work," she said.

After a little research, I learned that only 11% of pilgrims walk the full 800 km. The most popular starting point is the city of Sarria in Spain 115 km outside of Santiago de Compostela. If we started there, we could complete the pilgrimage in a week and receive an official certificate of completion, the

Compostela, for walking the minimum 100 km.

She was in!

I booked the flights and hostels (albergues) and we were ready to go in the summer of 2020. Then Covid happened, borders shut down around the world, and our trip was postponed indefinitely. The pandemic emphasized a motto I live by, "Do it today. Tomorrow is promised to no one."

As soon as the borders opened in 2022, we set out for the Camino with my teenage son, and our best friend's family and had an amazing adventure. I hope my story inspires readers to take a pilgrimage of their own sooner rather than later and helps them in their preparations.

Enjoy.

Pilgrims' names have been changed to protect their privacy.

CAMINO MAP

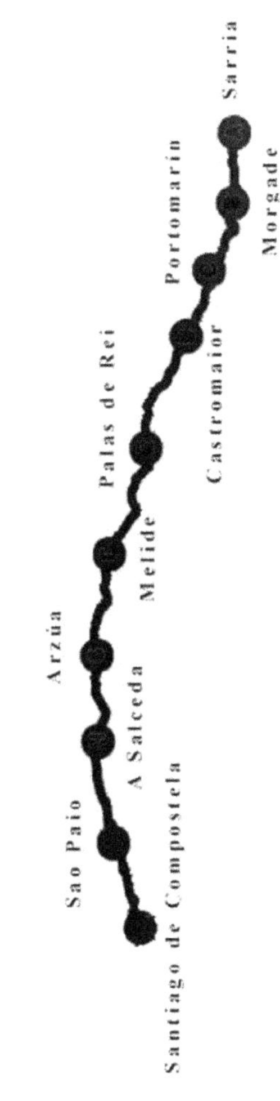

Sarria
Morgade
Portomarín
Castromaior
Palas de Rei
Melide
Arzúa
A Salceda
Sao Paio
Santiago de Compostela

DAY 1

Sarria

Cough, cough, cough.

Our first trial of the Camino: a heavyset man coughing and sneezing in the back of our bus from Toledo to Madrid. We had moved as far forward in the bus as we could, but I was worried. The Covid pandemic still dominated the news during the summer of 2022, so we hunkered down in our seats and hoped our masks did their jobs.

We had spent the last two days in Toledo during the city's magical Corpus Christi Festival. Now with my traveling companions, my wife Rosemary, my teenage son Adam, and three-fourths of the Davidson family - Roxanna and her two teenage daughters Olivia and Veronica, we were headed to Madrid to catch the afternoon train to Sarria where we would start walking the Camino. The fourth member of the Davidson family, father Louie, was still in Toledo waiting for his wife's and daughter's missing luggage.

As we boarded our fateful bus, an Air Canada representative called to say their luggage would be delivered to their Toledo hotel within the hour. The ladies were excited by the possibility of wearing fresh clothes, so Louie stayed behind. The only hitch was if he missed the next bus to Madrid, he would miss the day's train to Sarria.

For the next two hours, we rolled through the brown and yellow plains of central Spain, watching them bake under the country's second heatwave of the year, listening to the sick man, and waiting for Louie's call.

As we emerged from our sickly steel cocoon in Madrid, Louie called.

"Dang it!" Roxanna said. "Dang it! Dang it!"

Silence. Listening.

"Ok, Honey. See you soon." She thrust her phone into her Baggallini. “The luggage never arrived.” This was the second time Air Canada had said they would deliver the luggage only to fail.

“Did he catch the bus,” I asked.

“Yes,” she said, still peeved. Not only did their luggage have her and Olivia's clothing, but it also had all their Camino gear: ponchos, hiking clothes, hats, and other necessities. One thing we were learning in Spain was how to do without. And we had not even started the official Camino yet.

On the bright side, they had less to carry as I saw that we would have to cross one of the largest traffic circles I had ever seen as we exited the station. It had seven traffic lights and eleven entrances and exits. Of course, the taxi stand was on the far side of the circle. Huddling together, we set off, dodging traffic, and quickly forgetting about lost luggage.

Limbs attached, we entered a weird pecking order and discussion amongst a dozen taxi drivers about who would give us a ride. Based on the "winning" taxi drivers' resigned expressions, a bleach blond woman and deeply tanned man, it appeared that we had interrupted a fun conversation that no one had wanted to leave. Money vs. fun; job vs. relationships? Interesting.

We arrived at Chamartín Station with plenty of time to spare so I bought a latte at the station's coffee shop, Café de la Estación. I met my first Camino pilgrims here, Luke and Jasmine. Americans in their early 20s, blond hipster and long-haired brunette, they mirrored younger versions of me and my wife. He had flown in from Colorado and she from New Jersey and they taxied straight here. No time to sightsee in Madrid. They only had a week's vacation and then had to return home for work.

Clean backpacks, hiking clothes, and boots, they looked like they had just stepped out of a high-end sporting goods store. Like their clothes, I could tell they were a new item by the way they looked at each other, that sparkle in their eyes, and being exceedingly courteous around each other. Luke confessed this was only the second time they met in person. Starting out clean and fresh on a six-day Camino and ending mud splattered and sore would definitely tell them if their relationship would be long or very, very short-term. I wondered who proposed this adventure for a second date – Luke or Jasmine? I wish I knew how they fared, but they were headed to Lugo to walk the Camino Primitivo while we were headed to Sarria for the Camino Frances and would not see them again.

As I sipped my latte, two more pilgrims strode by. They stood in stark contrast to the two freshly minted lovebirds sitting next to us. The deeply tanned women, one Caucasian and one Asian, were in their 40s. Their stained boots, supple well-worn clothes, and numerous charms jingling on their packs told me they were veteran hikers. Their gear all looked right. No extra movement in their packs. Everything was secure. I had the strong sense they could easily knock out 40 kilometers a day while we struggled with 12.

Now compare the lovebirds and the veterans to our group: seven people with six roller suitcases, one backpack, one day pack, and four purses. And footwear? One pair of hiking shoes, two tennis shoes, and three sandals. Louie was the only one who wore his hiking boots every day and he wasn't here yet. Yep. We were a motley crew. No one could tell if we were going to the Costa del Sol for a day at the beach or novices heading for the Camino.

Three groups, all different in dress, equipment, and demographics. I wondered just how varied the pilgrims of the Camino would be.

As varied as tortilla españolas, perhaps? A

tortilla española is a traditional dish in Spain which at its most basic is an egg and potato omelet. However, some Spanish restaurants add onion inside; others add toppings using the tortilla like a pizza crust; others will cook them solid all the way through; and others will leave them runny in the middle. @spainrevealed has an interesting YouTube video on his search for the best tortilla in Madrid. So, when I bought a tortilla española in the station that had runny eggs, I knew it was not mistakenly undercooked. While it was good, I prefer mine cooked through.

Coffee check. Food check. Restroom...was unique. The wall to the entrance was covered by ivy and an attendant stood at a gate to collect one euro from each guest to enter. Inside the restroom was the sound of light rain and chirping birds. Very Zen.

Needs met, we gathered our bags and headed for the train. Louie appeared at that moment. He was a bit disheveled but relieved he had made it. The next train to Sarria wasn't for another six hours.

As it was, even though we were in line 30 minutes early, we were worried we would miss the train after all. The line to enter the two security checkpoints, one to the platform and one to the train, was already long. Within five minutes of us sitting down, the train pulled out. Close one.

I had booked our train and bus tickets directly through the operator's websites, Renfe and Alsa, months before we arrived. The sites were easy to navigate and had buttons to translate the pages into English. Since we were traveling during the peak tourist months of summer, I wanted to avoid sellouts. Train tickets are available to purchase three months in advance while bus tickets can be purchased further out. While in Spain, it appeared reserving bus tickets in advance was probably unnecessary, but trains seemed fuller and by booking in advance I was able to secure four seats around a table. The table made for a comfortable five-hour train ride allowing me to spread out my packed goodies, water, and journal.

"What are those," asked Roxanna, eyeing my sandwiches while she visited us from another part of the train.

"Peanut butter and jelly. Do you want one?"

"Oh, my goodness, my girls would die for one. They are so tired of eggs and potatoes." Her girls are vegetarians and found their food options extremely limited in Spain. She later reported that I was their hero for the day.

Hero status achieved, I sat back and watched the Spanish countryside whiz by. Leaving Madrid, cultivated fields of wheat and low dusty hills spread out around us. As we moved further north, the hills grew taller and more rugged. We passed through several tunnels, and after a particularly long one, we emerged into a landscape of tall green leafy trees, steep valleys, and green rivers. It was like another world. We travelled alongside the Miño River, fourth largest in Spain, crossed high bridges, and passed through the large city of Ourense, and on to the town of Monforte de Lemos where all the train passengers had to disembark. Due to construction on the rail line beyond the town, all the passengers transferred to buses to reach Sarria and points further north.

I had wondered if most of the pilgrims would be Americans as those were the only ones I had seen up to this point. However, stepping off the train, I was quickly disabused of that notion. Most of the passengers wearing Camino garb and gear around me spoke Spanish, French, or other European languages. Americans were definitely in the minority. According to the Oficina de Acogida al Peregrino (Pilgrim Reception Office), Americans only made up 5.94% of total pilgrims in 2019. So, if you want a European trip away from other American tourists, head for the Camino. Spain, Italy, and Germany supplied the most pilgrims that year. Aside from Europeans, I would meet people from Puerto Rico, India, Korea, Australia, and many other countries. It was truly a cosmopolitan road. But I am getting ahead of myself.

In Monforte de Lemos, I saw another distinct group of people, Galicians.

The people of Spain have roots to their towns and provinces going back hundreds or even thousands of years inlaying specific physical characteristics on many of its people. Before the Romans and Moors arrived in northwestern Spain, it was the land of the Celts, think bagpipes not castanets. Yet, when I think of Celtic stereotypes,

I picture red-haired, green-eyed, pale-skinned individuals. And when I think of Spaniards, I think of dark hair, dark eyes, and olive skin. I found most Galicians to be a combination of the two.

A young Galician woman yelling directions to transferring passengers was pale skinned, dark haired, and dark eyed. Many of the Galicians I would meet also had green eyes. I am painting a picture with a very broad demographic brush here. After all, her companion had blond hair to go with his dark eyes. I love how travel challenges my assumptions.

We boarded the buses under cloudy skies, sweating in the heat and humidity. After I stepped inside, the bus door closed behind me, and I heard Louie exclaim, "Come on!" He was outside the bus. No matter how much Roxanna pleaded with the bus driver, he refused to open the door. The Davidson's were separated again. Louie was not having the best of luck today.

We watched him board the bus behind us, shoulders slumped, and then we were off, winding through tree-covered hillsides for an hour before arriving in the town of Sarria.

Sarria is by far the most popular starting point to walk the Camino. According to caminoways.com, 26% of all pilgrims start here, 11% in St. Jean Pied de Port for the full 800km experience, and the rest from a dozen other locations including Portugal.

Why is Sarria the most popular starting point? First, to receive their Compostelas, pilgrims must walk at least 100 km to Santiago and Sarria is 112 km away. Second, Sarria is the gateway to Galicia. This means more trees, usually cooler than the rest of Spain, and relatively flat compared to the earlier stages of the full Camino. By no means is it easy, but pilgrims are not climbing the Pyrenees or crossing the shadeless Meseta. Final reason, is time. Most pilgrims walk the 112 km in five or six days, meaning they can complete their trip in a week like the young couple we met in Chamartin station. A pilgrim could fly in on a Saturday and return home the following Sunday, Compostela in hand.

However, we planned a nine-day Camino, walking an average of 12 km a day versus a typical pilgrim's 20 km. We were taking it slow. The adults in our group routinely walked 10,000 steps a day back home, about 8 km. I figured walking 12 km was only an extra 25% added to our daily walks, so no problem. I also figured 12 km would only take three to four hours a day, allowing us plenty of time to recover and leaving our afternoons free. Ha ha ha. Not to foreshadow too much, but according to my wife's Fitbit, we walked 200km over those nine days and Kompeed patches for blisters became one of my best friends.

We logged our first unplanned kilometer walking from the station to our albergue (hostel), La Casona de Sarria. Gray stone buildings lined the streets which were quite distinct from central and southern Spain where buildings where of brown stones or whitewashed. We passed a large supermarket and many stores and restaurants.

Pilgrims walked the streets, but not many, surprising me. Some writers had described hordes of pilgrims crowding the sidewalks. Not so today. That being said, our albergue was sold out, turning pilgrims away while we waited to check in.

Like our transportation, I had reserved all our lodging three months in advance. Booking.com allowed me to easily reserve all our apartments, albergues, and hotels on their website.

Many pilgrims like to book rooms as they go: the excitement of not being tied down to a fixed travel point each day. However, I like to leave little to chance. One pilgrim I met on the road said her group had planned on staying in a town further back on the Camino, but everything was booked when they arrived and had to walk an additional 10 km to find lodging. Most importantly, my wife had two requirements for our lodging: we had to have a private room and a private bathroom. There was no way I could guarantee those conditions without reservations. While I was able to secure private rooms throughout our journey, I was only able to secure a private bathroom eight out of ten nights.

La Casona De Sarria consisted of two buildings. The yellow one on Rúa Xela Arias housed the reception desk, downstairs dining room, and hotel-like rooms. The other, our building, was a long city block closer to the start of the Camino, 150 years old, and had a façade of typical gray Galician stone. It was exactly what I expected an albergue to look like. However, Adam did not appreciate staying in a historic building after staying in an ultra-modern Hyatt in Madrid and an apartment in Toledo with all the modern conveniences of home.

I agreed with Adam that there were some good things about modern buildings, specifically air conditioning. Since Galicia is usually cold and rainy, most lodging along the Camino did not have air conditioning. On a rare hot day in Galicia, like today, sleeping was a challenge.

This brings me to a unique feature of Galician accommodations. If a room does not have air conditioning, what would be the next choice to keep a room cool? The answer, windows. Every room we stayed in had windows that could be opened to allow in a breeze, but there were no window screens. I found that strange. Aside from saving money on screens and needing to have one window available to hang clothes (many Spanish apartments had clothes lines outside their windows), I didn't understand why lodgings wouldn't have screens. Wouldn't they be inundated with bugs? Surprisingly, they were not. Adam did see a fly and a baby spider which also lessened his appreciation of the room, but we were never bitten. Perhaps biting bugs in Galicia are like vampires and don’t enter homes unless invited.

At La Casona de Sarria, we met one of the coolest albergue owners of our trip, Marcela. Not only was she super friendly and helpful, but she also said for eight euros a person we could have the best breakfast on the Camino the next morning.

How could we turn down the best breakfast on the Camino.

Marcela was from Argentina. We would meet many business owners during our Spanish travels from other countries, for example: in Toledo, a woman from China who owned a traditional Spanish bodega complete with hanging legs of ham; in Cáceres, a German woman who owned a piso with her Spanish husband that they rented out; on the Camino, a couple from Northern California who owned an albergue and lived there during the summer months. The one thing they all had in common was a love of Spain: the food, the people, and the culture.

We bumped into Marcela three times during our late afternoon sojourns around town. One time, she carried groceries for tomorrow morning's mysterious breakfast. Another, she suggested the Italian restaurant Matías for dinner as the girls wanted pizza.

To get to Matías, we had to walk uphill to the old town of Sarria. The area had cobblestone streets, a couple of churches, restaurants, and a big photo-op sign that said SARRIA. This was another unplanned kilometer added to our Camino. See how easily the kilometers add up?

Matías had delicious food and the sweetest giant tomatoes any of us had ever eaten and they were served with fresh mozzarella slices. Their Pisqueña pizza was amazing: ham, bacon, mozzarella, mushrooms, tomato sauce, and cream.

I am sure those special tomatoes were used in the sauce. The vegetarian girls loved their margarita pizza. Everyone, except Adam, washed it all down with our drink of choice throughout Spain, tinto de verano. Tinto de verano is wine over ice, mixed with lemon soda. It was sweet and refreshing.

"Do you want a tinto de verano too, Adam?"

"No, Dad."

"Why not?"

"I just don't like the way alcohol makes me feel."

"What do you mean?"

"I just like to feel in control of myself. And when I drink, it's harder to do that."

I felt very proud of him at that moment. If you are wondering why I offered alcohol to my 19-year-old son, in Spain the legal drinking age is 16. We had shared our first alcoholic drink, and it turned out to be his last, when we were in Madrid.

Stuffed with pizza and tomatoes, we took a plethora of pictures throughout the old town and headed back toward our albergue. Halfway down the hill, I realized I had forgotten my sunhat at the Sarria sign and hurried back. Even though it was 7 pm, this was the hottest time of day during summer in Spain. Sweat ran off me in rivulets as I tried to catch up to my group. So much so, I took off my collared shirt and just wore my white tank top. I felt self-conscious as Spaniards appear to always dress nice, especially middle-aged men. But I felt for the first and only time in Spain, that I was overheating because I had unwittingly overexerted myself.

When I reached our group at the bottom of the hill, I downed my wife's bottle of water (mine was long gone) and took a breather. Then the collared shirt came back on, and Adam and I went into the wonderfully air-conditioned Coviran supermarket to buy water and snacks. The ladies all went to a sporting goods store in town to replace some of the Canadian Airlines-kidnapped necessities for the Camino.

Back at the albergue, I took a shower, changed clothes, and handwashed my sweaty items. This became my standard routine on the trip when we arrived at our lodgings: shower, put on fresh clothes, handwash dirty clothes, and hang them to dry. Almost every day the clothes would be dry by morning. The key was to handwash as soon as we arrived. If I waited until after dinner, the clothes could still be damp the next morning. Another tip, especially on rainy days: I would roll up the clothes in a towel for a minute after handwashing which helped absorb some of the water. It was a little trick I have used since coming home from the beach on the bus as a teenager.

While I made the peanut butter and jelly sandwiches for the next day in our albergue's communal kitchen, I spoke to a woman from Malaga who was walking the Camino with two friends. She had the dark eyes and well-tanned skin of the inhabitants of Southern Spain.

"Our kids are at camp, so we do the Camino. Have fun," she said in English.

"Have fun and meet great people," I said, spreading strawberry jelly on the bread.

Her friends drinking on the couch laughed.

"Have a Buen Camino," she said and then rejoined her friends.

It turned out the sandwiches were unnecessary. Numerous bodegas and cafes lined the Camino refueling us as needed. Lighter weight snacks like trail mix or a banana or a croissant taken from a morning's breakfast worked out great between stops. I carried those Sarria-premade sandwiches for three days before I finally threw the last one away, squished in the bottom of my daypack.

I was excited for tomorrow, and with the hot night, I tossed and turned, finally giving up at 5:15 am and prepared for our first walk and our promised amazing breakfast.

Tomorrow: And Away We Go!

DAY 2

Casa Morgade 12km

Marcela did not lie. She served up one of the most amazing breakfasts that I had ever had, let alone on the Camino!

Pancakes, chocolate-caramel topping, date marmalade, scrambled eggs, toast, serrano ham, prosciutto, bananas, oranges, kiwis, coffee, and more. She made everything from scratch from the jelly to the pancakes. Spanish and English rock songs played in the corner. When "Leaving, On A Jet Plane" by Bob Denver came on, all of us, including Marcela sang along at full volume.

Adam, totally embarrassed, ran up the stairs and outside the hotel and said he could still hear us. What an inspiring way to officially start our Camino.

When we finished breakfast, we were stuffed. If we kept eating like this, we would be rolling our way into Santiago de Compostela. Fortunately, we were not carrying our luggage.

There are two ways pilgrims can take their luggage on the Camino. First, transport it themselves. This is the most iconic way of completing the Camino: a pilgrim carrying a backpack with all their clothing and necessities. Props to Adam as he was the only person in our group to do it this way.

The second way is to hire a company to transport their luggage from albergue to albergue. In this way, pilgrims only carry what they need for the day's walk: water, snacks, raingear, etc. The rest of us opted for this method as most people in our party had never backpacked before. I hired Caminofácil before we left the United States, and for five euros per bag per day our luggage was always waiting for us when we arrived at our next albergue.

The luggage transfer service also helped ensure our mornings did not get away from us. Our bags had to be in the lobby by 8 am thereby providing us with a scheduled departure time each day. And it forced us to plan on what we needed for the day because once our bags were in the lobby, we were stuck with what we were wearing and carrying until we arrived at our next albergue.

What did we wear and carry for the first day? Our appearance was the epitome of doing the Camino in your own way. As we headed out into the bright sun, Roxanna and her girls wore dresses and skirts and had tied their rain jackets around their waists. Louie and I at least looked the part of “traditional” pilgrims: cargo pants, hiking shirts, and safari hats, and Louie even had a safari vest with at least a dozen pockets. I carried a small day pack and he carried all his families’ water and snacks in a large plastic grocery bag. Rosemary was a cross between a pilgrim and a city slicker: safari shirt and hat, yoga pants, and a Bagallini. Adam was the gray man: gray pants, gray t-shirt, black shoes, gray safari hat, and gray backpacker pack.

Booted up, my day pack filled with peanut butter and jelly sandwiches, water, rain gear, and first aid supplies, we were off, crossing the stone bridge that led out of Sarria and toward Santiago. It was the idyllic embarkation point for crossing into the emerald landscape of the Galician portion of the Camino. Today, we would walk 12 km to Morgade on a mix of dirt and small paved roads.

Ten minutes in, I noticed Roxanna and Olivia trailing our group.

"How are you two doing?"

"Olivia is feeling a little under the weather," Roxanna said.

"Too much breakfast?"

"No. Just tired, achy, a little congested," Olivia said.

My thoughts went back to the man coughing on the bus. Covid? Cold? Allergies?

"If she gets worse," Roxanna said, "we might have to take a taxi for the next leg."

Just then we caught up to Rosemary who was off to the side of the road bent over. She had had way too much breakfast she said, especially the rich chocolate-caramel pancake topping.

Well, that was an inauspicious start to our Camino.

I am glad to say that Olivia strengthened as the day progressed. Perhaps it was the beauty of the Camino: tree-shaded small roads, golden fields of wheat, and small stone hamlets. Or perhaps it was the dozens of "Buen Caminos" we received from our fellow pilgrims. Or perhaps it was the wonder of youth. Whatever the reason, by the time we reached the village of Barbadelo an hour later, she was walking at the front of our group with her sister.

Barbadelo, like most of the towns and villages along the Camino, was old, inhabited for over 1,000 years, and lined with crumbling buildings, giving it an air of ancient mystery, life, and death. The ruins were a reminder of how rural communities throughout Spain and the world were being depopulated as youth and others headed to the cities for more opportunities. At the village's heart stood a 12th-century, two-story church with a three-story tower surrounded by a graveyard with above ground tombs providing the finishing eerie touch. It would be a great setting for a supernatural film. I would not want to wander around here after dark.

During the day, it was easy for pilgrims to find their way. Iconic Camino de Santiago markers, pylons with yellow scallop shells painted on a blue background, stood wherever there was a fork in the road. The markers also indicated how many kilometers were left to reach Santiago.

The scallop shell has been associated with the Camino since pilgrims started making their way to Santiago in the 9th century. One interpretation of its design is that all roads (shell's ridges) lead to Santiago (the closed end of the shell). Another interpretation of their meaning by William Starkie in his, *The Road to Santiago*, was that the shells represented the ancient goddess Venus, and later the Romans used it as a charm against the evil eye. During the Middle Ages, the scallop shell could only be purchased in Santiago as proof a pilgrim completed their pilgrimage. Today, many pilgrims purchase their shells at the beginning of their journeys and hang them on their backpacks as they head toward Santiago. I had one swinging from my backpack that I had purchased in the United States and painted blue and yellow.

Other markers of the Camino were roadside shrines and donativos. Pilgrims created the shrines by leaving seashells, ribbons, and other mementos to mark their passage. Donativos were tables or stands where people set out food and/or water for pilgrims in exchange for a donation. At the first donativo we encountered, someone had set out bananas, apples, and water with a sign asking for donations. The organizer was nowhere to be seen.

Then there were the ruddy-brown cows, Rubia Gallegas. We saw lots of them. Usually they were in green fields, but in one instance, we had to squeeze past a rancher and his herd as they moved from one pasture to another. The Camino was very narrow here, or so it seemed as I passed the 1,500-pound animals with 2-foot-long horns. A flick of a cow's head and I would be making the evening news. Fortunately, they appeared accustomed to pilgrims as they passed us without a glance, no doubt daydreaming about the greener pastures just ahead. Rosemary thought they were “cool” and had no fear of snapping close-up selfies with them.

"Another picture, Mom?" Adam said. This, or "Another picture, Dad?" became his most frequent questions during our time in Spain. He wanted to finish each day's walk as soon as possible, while Rosemary and I wanted to store every moment we could on our phones.

"Yes, Dad, that's a cow."

"Adam, check out the view of the hills."

"It’s like the other one."

"Take a picture of me next to this marker."

"I took a picture of you at the last one."

He did not understand my goals of wanting to absorb every experience, to talk to strangers, or just be there.

"Let's get to the next hostel, so we can relax," he said. He saw a goal to accomplish, an objective to complete, a challenge to overcome. I understood that mindset. As a teenager, I remember being impatient with my mom when she would want to check out stores or historical sites for what seemed like forever. Now I was that parent, and my son was that teenager. To be fair to Adam, even my mom and wife routinely told me to move on as I could spend hours in a museum or hanging out at a coffee shop. I am sure he could have easily walked the 112 km from Sarria to Santiago in the five days it usually took walkers versus the nine we were taking.

To Adam's continued annoyance, we stopped at our first Camino café an hour after taking pictures with the cows. My morning drink of the Camino was a café latte sin lactosa. I was happy to discover that almost every place that served coffee also had lactose free milk, as I am lactose intolerant. Spain has one of the highest dairy-intolerances in Europe according to Just-food.com, hence the prevalence of lactose-free dairy products there. Sorry vegetarians, while they did serve lactose-free milk, to the girls' disappointment, not every place had plant-based milk alternatives.

A final note on coffee in Spain, almost all the espresso machines I saw along the Camino had the Italian coffee brand Lavazza stamped on them. Aside from selling a good espresso, the company must have the best salesperson in the world. I could imagine the conversation with the sales manager.

"Valentina, we want to send you on a sales trip to sell our espresso machines in Spain."

"Sounds fantastic! For how long?"

"Eight weeks."

"Even better."

"But there is a catch."

"What's that?"

"To show your understanding of our customers, you have to walk all 800 kilometers of the Camino Francés to make sure you meet them all."

"Perfetto! I won't let you down."

And the imaginary Valentina did not.

To Adam's relief, we only stayed at the café for fifteen minutes. But those fifteen minutes and caffeine infusion energized me. The weather had grown warmer, and the sun beamed down upon us. Fewer pilgrims walked the road now than when we started. We were headed to Casa Morgade only 12 km from Sarria, but most pilgrims were headed to Portomarín 22 km away. They either departed Sarria earlier than we did or did not stop for cows and coffee so they could reach Portomarin by lunch time.

As we rounded a hill at 1 pm, I saw a long two-story stone building on the left-hand side of the road all by itself. It was Casa Morgade, our destination for the day! It was like arriving at Shangri-La. We had completed our first trek! Everyone felt relieved at reaching our destination. We now knew what a 12km walk would be like.

Aside from our albergue, Casa Morgade also had a gift shop, restaurant, and bar. As we registered inside the gift shop, I was pleased to see our luggage sitting in the lobby on the other side of a doorway. Caminofácil had come through.

Like most albergues we stayed in, Casa Morgade appeared to be a family-run operation. Most of the staff, in the gift shop, kitchen and our waiter, had similar facial features and a couple of children related to the gift shop clerk/receptionist hung out in the store. How did I know the children were related? While checking in, she reprimanded the boy as only a parent does – smiling at us, barely a glance in the boy's direction, a quick serious utterance of the boy's name out the side of her mouth, boy stops, and back to smiling and talking to us. That quick parental reprimand while talking to other adults I know well, using it often while raising my sons. It must be a universal parental technique.

Adam had no complaints about the rooms here. I had to rent him his own room as Morgade only had single and double rooms. Not only did he have his own room, but the white-painted walls made the room look more modern than the stone one of La Casona de Sarria. He was so comfortable here, that when he saw a fly in his room this time, he said it did not bug him. "It's my friend, George."

For lunch, Morgade had a dining patio with views far off to the west over hills, fields, and trees. Unfortunately, the sun was out in full force and there was no sun protection. So, we ate lunch at Morgade's little dining area across the street under orange umbrellas. Their ice-cold sangria hit the spot. Their tourist menu's pork cutlet, french fries, and salad were just what I needed after our walk.

As we ate and watched the few late-traveling pilgrims walk on to Portomarin, I spoke with a couple at the next table. Ray and Jessica had started their Camino in Sarria and were taking ten days to complete their Camino just like us. But unlike us, they had a travel agent make all of their arrangements including luggage transfers.

"I just turned 80 and wanted to walk the Camino," Ray said.

"60?", I said.

"No, 80," he said with a smile.

I looked at him again. He had white hair, wrinkles, well-tanned skin, but his forearms and calves were well muscled, and he spoke strong and clear. I looked at his wife sitting next to him. She smiled. She looked younger than him, 60s or early 70s, so I knew he wasn't putting me on. He had retired this year after working as an engineering contractor in England his entire life. Now he wanted to travel and experience as much as possible. We would constantly run into Ray and Jessica for the next nine days and became good friends. They were in amazing shape and frequently wound up ahead of us, or at least me, on the Camino.

After lunch, I handwashed my clothes at the albergue's washing station and hung them on their clotheslines. I met Park and his wife who were doing the same.

"My wife and I started walking 28 days ago from St. Jean-Pied-de-Port," Park said. "We will finish in 32 days."

"That means you will walk 100 km in the next three days," I said, impressed.

"Yes, it will be hard." He glanced down at his ankle. I noticed an icepack wrapped around it. "I sprained my ankle from too much walking with a heavy pack."

"Are you going to be okay?"

"I just retired from the Korean army, so I am ok. But my wife," he said, then paused and continued beaming. "I am very proud of her. She hasn't done anything like this before. She is a very strong woman."

After they finished the Camino, they would travel to Barcelona for a few days and then on to Rome to meet up with their college-aged kids and stay in Europe for another 2 months. He was living his dream now, he said, as he had worked too much in his life.

I was seeing a common theme here.

In the lobby, I found Adam where he was working on his novel in the Templar journal he had purchased in Toledo. His story had been ruminating in his mind for some time, and only with this journal had he started writing it down. He was only using it for notes, he said, not committing the story to paper yet. I look forward to the day he does, so I can read it.

Rosemary and I had thick vegetable soup and dipping bread for dinner as we were still full. After our breakfast experience, we were cautious about overeating. Being a teenager, Adam had no problem finishing off a delicious steak chop aka ribeye. It was his third steak chop since we had been in Spain, so I had to give him a reality check. He could not order the most expensive item on the menu at every meal unless he planned on paying for it. He ordered few steaks after this.

The sunset of red and yellow was gorgeous. Dark thin clouds rolled in adding to its beauty and foretold another experience, our first Camino rain.

Tomorrow: The Town Rebuilt on a Mountain Top

DAY 3

Portomarín 10 km

The night's rain had left behind a chilly morning. Spain's second heatwave of the year had finally broken. Even better, the rain had stopped by the time we finished breakfast, leaving behind the smell of wet concrete and the sight of glistening green foliage. Everyone but the girls wore long sleeves and pants today. The girls wore dresses, Olivia because her luggage was still missing and had no other option and Veronica because she wanted to. They donned their rain jackets atop their dresses in their only acknowledgement to the change in weather.

So far our feet were doing well. Veronica had chaffing where her sandal had rubbed against the side of her barefoot yesterday, but moleskin had solved that issue. I only had one blister, and that was from walking the hilly cobblestone streets of Toledo two days earlier in tennis shoes and cotton socks.

Since I changed to wool socks and hiking shoes, and affixed Kompeed patches to any hotspots that developed on my feet going forward, I avoided any new blisters from forming the rest of the Camino.

Today's walk was filled with lots of "lots." Lots of trees, clouds, short fences, moss-covered low stone walls, walking sticks, cemeteries with above-ground tombs, and "Buen Caminos" offered to and received from fellow pilgrims.

We reached the 100 km marker which indicated our distance from Santiago de Compostela and took our obligatory pictures. 100 km is the minimum distance a pilgrim has to walk in order to obtain their Compostela. Since we had already walked over 15 km to this point, I was proud that we were walking more than the bare minimum to achieve our goal.

A nearby house had an elaborate spread of food and drinks for donativos: breads, fruit, coffee, and chaffing dishes with hot food. It had a beautiful courtyard filled with colorful flowers: purple, red, pink, and white. Rosemary chatted with the 70-year-old owner who told her he liked seeing all the different pilgrims and setting out food gave him a purpose every day.

A little further down the trail, the rain began. Everyone donned their ponchos or rain jackets, except Adam. He said it wasn't real rain. True, it was more of a steady drizzle, but he was, in my mind not his, soaked within thirty minutes.

We passed an isolated store selling goods and

gear as well as at least 80 different hand-painted scallop shells hanging on its front door. Some shells were whimsical, others heavy with religious symbolism, some with pilgrims, and some with rainbows. If we didn't have shells already, I am sure we would have bought some.

Then we stopped at the House of Flags. It was a place Rosemary had seen on a YouTube video. The building had streamers of flags hanging from countries throughout the world. The owners from Northern California sold coffee and snacks and would place a hot wax seal in our Credencial del Peregrino book for a fee.

To prove that a pilgrim has completed the Camino, a pilgrim obtains a Credencial del Peregrino at the beginning of their journey, usually at an albergue, church, or store, and then each day they must obtain stamps from two different locations.

The House of Flags hot wax stamp was a gimmick. Travel books warned us not to pay for any stamps as they are supposed to be free. However, I did enjoy seeing the bronze-colored wax heated and poured onto our Credencials and an old-style stamp pressed into it creating a seal. Unfortunately, by the time we reached Santiago, they had all broken off. This could have been a disaster if we had not obtained a third stamp that day when we saw the seals breaking.

Just before the Miño River and Portomarín, we reached a four-way fork in the road with a rough map of the area.

"You should go left," a pilgrim in black rain pants and jacket told us as he rested with his group.

"Why is that?"

"The right road is shorter, but steeper down to the river. In the rain, the road is very slick."

"Thanks for the tip."

"Also, don't take the first right down the left road, you want to take the second right."

I was not sure how he knew this. Had he scouted the route beforehand? Or was he a veteran of the Caminos and knew what to expect? We followed his advice and made it to the river easily. Along this alternate route, we saw a fat four-inch black slug on the rain-slicked dirt road. It must have felt like a celebrity with all the photos we took of him. We also saw where the first turn from the left fork met our road, and it looked like a muddy goat trail. I am glad we listened to all the pilgrim's suggestions.

From our side of the river, we had a sweeping view of the high bridge that led to Portomarín. The town was whitewashed like those in Southern Spain and its original location by the river dated back to the Romans. However, the town that we saw on the hill was the new Portomarín. In the 1960s, Dictator Francisco Franco built a dam on the Miño River, flooding the town, forcing the citizens to relocate the city to the top of the hill. Like the temple of Abu Simbel in Egypt when the Nile was dammed, the town was reconstructed brick by brick on a nearby hill. When the river level was low, as it was today, the ruins of the old town and original lower Roman bridge could be seen.

After taking many pictures, we crossed the new bridge, and then walked up 52 stairs into the city. Don't miss the large Instagrammable sign with the word PORTOMARÍN at the city's entrance like we did. We were so eager to find our apartment, that we didn't notice it until our evening walk and wondered how on earth we missed it.

Portomarín is the traditional stop after Sarria, about 22 km away, so finding lodging can be challenging. When I looked for a place to stay three months in advance, I could not find an albergue with a private room and bathroom that could accommodate three people. As a result, I rented an apartment.

The Apartamentos Ruliña would be our most expensive lodging on the Camino but was well worth it. While the outside was a plain white multi-storied apartment building, inside it had all the modern luxuries of home: tv, air conditioning, washing machine, and full kitchen. It was also in a great location, only a couple blocks from the main street and had a supermarket on the building's bottom floor. The young man in charge of cleaning and reception also provided a laundry drying service after we washed our clothes in our apartment's washing machine. No handwashing today!

After settling in, we ate lunch at Restaurante Perez which overlooked the Miño river, bridge, and edge of town. We also secured the one porch table that had just enough wooden awning to protect us from the rain that came and went throughout our meal. All the other patio tables were soaked. On this dreary day, I ordered a bowl of warm lentils and huevos con chorizo. Unlike the spicy chorizo mixed into scrambled eggs at Mexican restaurants back in Los Angeles, I was served a mild sausage sitting next to two over easy eggs. Not what I was expecting. I chopped the chorizo up and mixed it with the yokes, but it was not the same. The veal, cod, pulpo, and other plates we ate were all tasty.

After lunch, Rosemary and I dropped off Adam and our traveling companions and then explored Portomarín. First, we visited the rebuilt San Juan church. The 12th century church rose dramatically from the center of a wide-open concrete plaza. It was a giant rectangle, no flying buttresses, arches, or soaring towers. Above its front door was a large rose window, but my favorite feature stood just outside the church on the left: a whimsical statue of a priest carrying an umbrella in acknowledgement to Galicia's trademark weather.

On a nearby side street was a large six-paneled mural. The first panel depicted Saint James in his stone boat on his way to Spain. The fourth was a road going over hills, no doubt the Camino. But the meanings of the panel with a man carried by flying clams, a horse in water, a satchel and a cup, and a rooster and a chicken, stumped me. They were all very colorful.

In nearby Parque Antonio Sanz, we sat on

a bench and watched a white dog running and jumping like a maniac nonstop around the park in a long circle. It was fun watching him and his owner, a young man, egging him on. Then the dog ran behind some bushes and emerged covered in mud. Of course, at that moment, the rest of the man's family arrived and an older man in a suit admonished the dog for being dirty.

Portomarín's main street, Calle de Compostela, was lined by arched walkways with a variety of stores, pharmacies, markets, and an ice cream parlor - Xeou! The ice cream parlor lured Adam out of the apartment and there were a lot of happy chatty teenagers hanging about. When Adam went in for ice cream, he got appraising looks from a couple of young ladies who were ordering behind him. Unfortunately, Adam said he did not notice. He said being unable to speak and understand Spanish made him feel unsure of himself and uncomfortable interacting with those around him. While the Camino hosts people from around the world and most locals speak some English, being able to speak some Spanish can lead to richer interactions. However, being able to speak the local language, like Rosemary does, doesn't prevent a person from committing a cultural faux pas.

"Disculpe, señora."

Rosemary stopped placing nectarines in the plastic bag she was holding. We were in the supermarket in our apartment building.

"Sí, señor?" she said to the employee wearing a

white apron at the end of the produce area.

"No," he pointed at the fruit in her hand shaking his head.

I realized what the problem was. In smaller markets in Spain, the employees are the ones who pick and bag your produce. This happened to be one of those places. Oops. The proprietor proceeded to bag our fruit and veggies. Trusting others to pick and bag my produce was a strange concept for me because in America the custom is to pick and bag all our own produce. Yet, when Spanish proprietors did pick my produce, I only received one bad piece, and this was in Granada weeks later. I could live with only one bad nectarine during my entire trip.

For dinner, we stayed in our apartment eating ham, bread, and fruit from the market.

I had my best night's sleep on the Camino so far. With no computer to waste away my evenings, or crazy work hours, I would sleep by 10 and wake up at 6. It was the first regular sleep schedule in what seemed like years. Nice.

Tomorrow: Losing Adam

DAY 4

Castromaior 8 km

As we prepared to leave the apartment, there was a knock at the door.

"Rosemary," Roxanna said, "do you have extra clothes the girls can borrow?"

"What's wrong?"

"It's going to be really cold today and they have nothing warm to wear."

Roxanna and Olivia's luggage with their warm clothes still floated around Spain with Air Canada. Fortunately, Rosemary had extra pants and hiking shirts in her large rollaway we were shipping from albergue to albergue. Thank goodness for Caminofácil! When we met downstairs, Rosemary and the girls looked like triplets except for different colored rain jackets and Veronica wearing sandals. Yes, Veronica walked the entire Camino, rain or shine, in sandals.

Layering my Smartwool t-shirt, safari shirt, and

Frogg Togg rain jacket, I was good for every cool morning from here to Santiago. In the afternoon or on warmer days, I swapped the Smartwool t-shirt for a tank top or wicking athletic shirt.

Each day on the road, the number of pilgrims we saw increased. We ran into Ray and Jessica again and another couple we had met at Casa Morgade, Hugo and Sofia.

"Before my brother died," Hugo said, "I told him I would walk the Camino for him. That was twenty years ago."

"That's wonderful you are doing this," I said. "Why did you wait 20 years?"

A pained look crossed his face. "Work, life, other things." He gave a rueful smile. "Then I had a heart attack last year and knew I had to fulfill my promise soon."

I looked him over, concerned.

He laughed. "I am fine. I just have to take a lot of breaks."

I was inspired by what the human spirit could accomplish: Hugo had a heart attack last year, Ray was 80, and Park had a sprained ankle and yet they were all walking the Camino. I was doubly grateful for my relatively good health and having the opportunity to walk the Camino now at the young age of 50.

We stopped only once this morning on our way to Castromaior at Hostería de Gonzar's café. They had cute mugs that said, "Por que no hoy?" ("Why not today?"). Since the cafe was the first available restroom since Portomarín, 6 km away, it was very popular. However, in order to use the restroom, a person had to buy something, much like a "restroom for customers only" policy in the U.S. While in line, the owner told Adam he had to leave since he hadn't ordered anything. Fortunately, Rosemary was behind him and told her he was with us, and we had just ordered our usual morning lattes and pastries. Unfortunately for Adam, there were no to go cups, so we would be here for a while. He was itching to leave, so Rosemary told him to go on ahead to Castromaior. Off he went.

Casa Perdigueira, our albergue for the night, was a lot closer than we had expected. It was on the outskirts of Castromaior, closer to Sarria by 4 km. Now, instead of walking 12 km today and 12 km the next day, we only walked 8 km today and would be walking 16 km the next day. I looked forward to the challenge, however others in our party were not so keen about an extra hour of walking.

When we arrived in Castromaior, Adam was nowhere to be seen. Had he turned off earlier on a wrong road? Had he gone ahead? We waited fifteen minutes at Café-Bar O Castro near our albergue and there was still no sign of him. I tried calling him, but the call went straight to voicemail. I had refused to pay the $300 my phone carrier wanted for an international phone plan to use in Spain, so Adam had turned his phone off while we walked. I had no way of contacting him. I felt like I was in the Dark Ages.

Searching, Rosemary walked ahead while I backtracked in case he had gone the wrong way. I found Hugo, Sofia, Ray, and Jessica and they said they had not seen him. I went further back, but no luck. I tried calling Rosemary, but her phone was off too. After 20 minutes, I returned to the café, refilled on water, then headed after Rosemary. She was also coming back with no luck. I continued on.

Five minutes further down the road, I saw Adam walking back with a big smile on his face.

"Where were you?" I said.

"I was waiting in the next town. I didn't realize the hostel was so close. Then your friends found me (Hugo and the others) and told me you were looking for me, and you were upset."

I admit, I was.

"Then," he continued, "when I was coming back, six girls hanging out at a pizza place asked me to join them. But I said I couldn't because I was looking for my parents."

I felt bad causing my son to miss an opportunity to hang out with women his age. We returned to the café in silence. But once there, everyone was relieved and happy to see Adam back, and then we checked into our albergue.

Casa Perdigueira had four rooms with a great view of the farmland and trees that bordered the hamlet. Our group occupied the three upstairs rooms and a female pilgrim stayed in the downstairs room. There was a shared bathroom on the top floor and one on the bottom. The upstairs bathroom met

Rosemary's standard as a private bathroom as only our group used it.

Side note: the pilgrim who stayed in the room on the first floor wrote an online complaint about us being too noisy. Ha! I guess 50-year old's having to go to the bathroom throughout the night was very disturbing. Curiously, she did not complain about the hamlet's mooing cows that had to be as loud as we were.

Speaking of cows, I assumed that we would be served ultra-fresh milk on the Camino due to all the dairy farms in Galicia. Unfortunately, the café owners told us the farms shipped all their milk to big producers to be processed, packaged, and sold. None was sold to the local restaurants.

After settling in our rooms, Rosemary, Adam, and I lunched on bocadillos at Café-Bar O Castro while Roxanna's family took a taxi to the main area of "town" hoping for more vegetarian options. They ate at the pizza place where Adam had spoken to the female pilgrims earlier. When we passed by it the next day, it was crowded with high schoolers and college students. It appeared to be the young people's hangout in the area.

Back at the Café O Castro, we had an enjoyable conversation with the owner Silva and her cousin Olivia who owned Casa Perdigueira. Olivia said she always lived in the house until she turned it into an albergue in 2019. And then Covid hit in 2020 and she had to shut down for two years.

I had heard similar Covid stories all along the

Camino. After a record-setting 300,000 pilgrims made the trek in 2019, people like Olivia opened new businesses along the Camino. When Covid hit in 2020, many owners sold their businesses or went bankrupt. As a result, there were fewer lodging and dining facilities open than there were pre-Covid. Fortunately for us, Olivia's and Silva's comfortable businesses were up and running.

Olivia told me she hoped for a good 2022. She would get her wish. 2022 would set a new record with over 400,000 pilgrims completing the Camino.

Since only Olivia and another of her cousins worked at the café, we had to place orders for dinner during lunch and reserve a time to eat. While the options were only beef or chicken, the food was good, and served with healthy portions of meat, french fries, salad, and bread. Unfortunately, the girls were limited to yet another tortilla española to go along with the sides.

Like at isolated Casa Morgade, I enjoyed being in a place where there was nothing to do except relax, eat, drink, write, and talk to people. The history of the trail, the stone buildings, and the fact that guests all arrived on foot gave me a different feeling from staying at a bed and breakfast in the United States. It almost felt like a real-life Dungeons and Dragons' adventure without the monsters. A traveler comes into a town's only inn and speaks to the barkeep and fellow travelers to catch up on the latest gossip and to hear stories of places far away.

I swapped stories with fellow pilgrims Anthony

and David who joined me for a drink in the afternoon as I was writing my day's notes at an outside table. Anthony had a strong East Coast accent from his home city of Philadelphia. He had started his Camino in St. Jean Pied de Port in France and crossed the Pyrenees on his way to Santiago, walking 25 to 30+ km a day. He would meet his wife in Santiago and then walk with her to Finisterre. She would have started at the beginning with him, but he wanted to walk the first part on his own. He elaborated no further, but the glint in his eye indicated going solo was his choice, not hers.

David was also a solo pilgrim. Tall and dark-haired, he had a heavy Australian accent. The three of us must've sounded like a bizarre chorus of English-speakers.

David had started his Camino deep in France at Le Puy. After walking 30 days and 700 km to St. Jean Pied de Port, he was now completing the 800 km of the Camino Francés. He had a superior air about him for having started in Le Puy and did not think much of me starting in Sarria. How do I know? As soon as I said where I started, I saw the light of interest in his eyes dim and his attention remained focused on Anthony during the rest of our conversation. Fortunately, Anthony had no pretentions, talking as if we were all longtime friends in a Philly pub.

I learned that everyone's Camino is different. My advice is to walk the Camino your own way and don't compare yourself to others' expectations. The only stories of people having an overall negative experience on the Camino that I heard of were those who thought it had to be done a certain way.

One Instagrammer I followed, started off super excited, but when she reached the Meseta portion of the Camino in the middle of a heatwave, she was miserable. She decided to hop on a bus to Leon, knocking off 10 days of walking and thereby shortening each future day's walk. She was so happy making that choice, she said. She would have done it sooner but had felt pressure to walk the entire Camino the "right" way.

Another Instagrammer, decided to leave the Camino Francés after a week of walking and hit the north coast of Spain, sunbathing and staying in nice hotels. She also remarked on her happiness in taking control of her journey and being free from others' expectations.

Unfortunately, another Instagrammer who was frustrated with life in the U.S., embarked on the Camino from St. Jean Pied de Port to escape all the negativity she felt back home and recenter herself. She was a good writer, and I really enjoyed her posts. But when she arrived in Sarria, she started posting how angry she was at having to share the trail with people who were not doing the "real" Camino. She had returned to her frustrated mentality that she had tried to escape in the United States. I felt sad for her after all the pain and sacrifice she had gone through to complete the Camino, only to wind up filled with frustration toward others at the end of her journey. She actually used the word hate to describe her fellow pilgrims.

Reader, if you only take one thing from my book and are planning to walk the Camino, I implore you to make the journey your own. Enjoy every moment, whatever that means to you. If something is not working, don't be afraid to take a detour, change things up - faster or slower, and know that everyone has different goals and expectations.

Tomorrow: The Unexpected Longest Day

DAY 5

Palas de Rei 16 km

The walk today was all about drinks and useful tools.

The batido de platano at Café-Bar O Castro was a welcome dietary change. It was only blended bananas and milk, but after eggs, potatoes, and fried food for days, the vegetarian girls had big smiles as they drained their glasses.

The weather was even colder today and would rain off and on for the next two days. My roomy rain jacket that fit over my day pack, rain pants, and waterproof boots worked like a dream keeping me and my gear dry. Adam still didn't think it was real rain. While he covered his backpack with its rain shell, his poncho stayed inside, making him quite soggy when we arrived at our next albergue.

Leaving Castromaior, we detoured through the ruins of Castro de Castromaior, a walled town founded in the 5th Century BC. The inhabitants abandoned it in the 1st Century BC when the Romans arrived. While there was a historical marker near the Camino for the turn off, there were no other informational signs and no path to walk through the ruins. To cross them, visitors had to walk atop the moss- and lichen-covered ruins laid out in geometric shapes where buildings once stood. The stormy skies above the ruins made for amazing pictures. And while it was a detour, much to Adam's angst, the Camino wrapped around the Castro, so the visit added less than a half hour to our walk.

We came upon a café with awesome thick drinking chocolate between Castromaior and Ligonde. Unfortunately, I did not write down the name and could not find it online afterwards. The blue and white mug the chocolate was served in said, Cafés El Globo Artesanos Del Café Desde 1965, but that was not the name of the café.

Veda, a young woman from India, had ordered the drinking chocolate after hearing us exclaim about it and agreed it was amazing. She was currently working on her master's in electrical engineering in Munich, Germany.

"My Dad said I shouldn't go to Germany," she said. "It would be too tough for you. So, I went."

"Good for you," Rosemary said.

"When I told him I was thinking about walking the Camino, you know what he said?"

"I can only imagine," Rosemary said.

"I couldn't do it because it would be too hard." She smiled. "So, I hopped on a plane to Sarria and here I am."

I loved her Dad's reverse psychology to motivate his daughter to push herself. Behind her super-friendly appearance, I could see that inner fire to accomplish anything she desired.

Further along, an Australian pilgrim told me that he and his wife do walks around the world. I was intrigued. There are other walks, other Caminos? I knew about hikes like the Pacific Crest Trail, The Inca Trail, and Appalachian Way but nothing like the Camino with food and accommodations setup specifically for walkers outside of Spain. He said he and his wife had walked across three national parks in England and completed two walks in Japan: the Japan Way (Tokyo to Kyoto) and a walk near Osaka past numerous shrines. I am excited to research these other walks as potential trips in the future.

Today was the most crowded day so far on our Camino and would only get more so as we closed in on Santiago de Compostela. A big reason for the congestion came from school groups now appearing on the road. Most were Spanish and some students carried provincial or national flags. The students joked, talked, or sang bringing a youthful vitality to the experience. One French school group sang loud and proud.

Don't worry that you might be stuck in the middle of a group of teenagers for long periods of time. They were fast, like Adam fast. I would be walking along in peaceful silence, then hear them approach, exchange “Buen Caminos” as they passed me, and then they were gone, and I would return to my contemplative silence, sometimes wondering where their schools were located and thinking about the conversations I overheard.

A few of the older high school groups carried their packs but were in the minority. Most bussed their luggage ahead to their next stop. The students had their very own Caminofácil. Carrying packs or not, what a great adventure for these students.

We arrived in Palas de Rei after five hours of walking, 9:30 am-2:30pm, 16km. We were tired, wet, and hungry. The modern-looking town felt dreary and downtrodden in the drizzling rain. The streets were empty, and everything but the restaurants were closed since we arrived at siesta time. Hosts at two restaurants couldn't care less if we ate there, and where we did eat, our waiter kept disappearing. The vibe was so different here versus all the other places we visited in Spain. Perhaps it had to do in part with a shrinking town mentality. Palas de Rei's population had dropped by half in the last 40 years from 6,398 in 1981 to 3,316 in 2021 according to citypopulation.de. Adding to the town’s unhappy feel, we also saw our first anti-Spain graffiti here.

There are many regional independence movements throughout Spain. Perhaps the most internationally well-known are Catalonia's political efforts and the Basque's ETA's bombings from the 1960s to 1990s. When I was a student in Spain in 1992, I kicked some cardboard boxes on the street and my Spanish friends reproached me. Not for making a mess, but because they truly believed there could have been a bomb inside. Fortunately, the last independence-related bombing was over a decade ago, but the desire for independence from Spain's central government for many people remains.

An emblem of a green horse at an entry way of a large multi-story apartment building identified our day's hostel, O Cabalo Verde. Of all the places we stayed in, this one felt most like what I imagined a hostel to be: bunkbeds, young people, and separate bathrooms. Walking up the narrow stairs to the second floor, we checked in with a young male receptionist. He was happily checking in two young backpacking women. When he checked us in, he gave us a key to our bathroom which was down the hall and told us not to touch the fourth bunkbed so he wouldn't have to wash the linens.

Speaking of washing, Rosemary was happy there was a washer and dryer on the premises to wash her and Adam's clothes. I still handwashed my clothes and used my trusty rope to hang dry them in our room, bunk to bunk. Yes, I touched the rail of the fourth bunk. Oops. I have a fear of my clothes shrinking if they are put in a dryer. My wife says I am paranoid. Am I?

While I handwashed my clothes at the sink on the third-floor patio, I met a Spanish man travelling with his family. He was in his mid-40s with black hair and a neat, clipped beard.

"Do you go fishing?" I said when I learned that he lived in the port city of Cádiz.

"Yes," he said.

"What do you catch?"

"Lubina." (Sea bass)

I felt a twinge of excitement at the prospect of catching fish in Spain.

"In Los Angeles," I said, "a fisherman can purchase a spot on a big boat that carries 40 to 80 fishermen to fish for the day. Is there a similar thing in Cádiz?"

"No, there is nothing like that. You either have to have a boat or go on your friends' boat."

That quelled my excitement, as it appeared fishing was a very exclusive activity here.

Aside from my trusty rope for hanging clothes, another useful item I brought on this trip was sports tape. I used it to secure our Caminofácil tags to our luggage each morning, to tape down the inner sole of Adam's shoe that had come apart, and to attach lamb's wool to blisters on the bottom of his foot and heel.

I learned about using lamb's wool for blisters from YouTuber Rob's Camino. He said not only does the wool provide an extra layer between a walker's skin and their footwear, the lanolin from the wool also acts as a soothing balm to sore areas. Adam testified to that fact as he said it really helped alleviate the pain as he walked.

Rob also gave me a great tip about bringing two types of underwear for men. No matter how comfortable one type is, wearing a second type every 3rd or 4th day, boxer vs. briefs for example, can help prevent chaffing as it will rub a different area giving the other area a welcome respite.

After three days, I decided upon my favorite go-to-app for navigation: the Buen Camino app. I had been downloading a Google map each night using my hostel's wi-fi but found myself using the Buen Camino app most of the time. It was clearer in terms of distance travelled, yet to travel, and locating our hostels.

People were up late in Palas de Rei. At 10:45 pm, guys played soccer outside and a Spanish pop song blared from a bar or someone's flat. I missed the peace of our isolated stays in Castromaior and Morgade. But after our unexpected long day, when my head hit the pillow, I was out.

Tomorrow: The Happy Town

DAY 6

Melide 14km

The day started off great! A bakery, Panadería Fraga, around the corner from our albergue just had their delivery of baked goods and the employee was still placing them in the display cases from their carts. Their warm wheaty aroma filled the store. What caught my eye were the empanadas. Empanadas in Los Angeles meant hand-sized, crescent-shaped pastries filled with a variety of ingredients. A Galician empanada was a flat, pizza-sized pastry also filled with a variety of ingredients. Due to its size, it was sold to customers in slices, much like a pizza. I ordered a slice filled with tomato sauce, pancetta, and sausage. The vegetarians had slices filled with mushrooms. I also ordered a slice of apple tart for later. All were super fresh, delicious, and walking friendly.

As we left Palas de Rei, we withdrew money from an ATM. Many US banks have partner banks in Spain where customers can make fee-free withdrawals. Unfortunately, my bank's partner did not have an ATM in the town. While I was able to withdraw money, both the foreign bank and my bank charged me fees.

Fortunately, we rarely needed cash. Almost every business along the Camino accepts credit cards. A Spain guidebook published in 2019 spoke about the need for cash as "few places along the Camino had card readers." It showed how commerce can change so quickly. Perhaps Covid increased the acceptance of credit cards to minimize physical contact with customers. Unlike in the U.S., businesses in Spain will never physically touch your credit card. One business owner told me that it is against the law for them to do so. Covid-era restriction or security reason? I don't know. However, when I give my credit card to my waiter in the U.S. now, I think about how vulnerable I make myself to scams.

Still, there are a few establishments along the Camino that are cash only, especially the pop-up fruit and snack stands, so I found having some euros useful.

After walking an hour, I stopped for a slice of tortilla española and my usual morning latte at the gray stone Albergue Abrigadoiro in San Xulián do Camino. The tiny hamlet had a cross in the center of its main road and a 12th-century church with a beautifully painted statue of Santiago inside.

After another hour, I ordered a glass of machine-squeezed fresh orange juice at a café. Like the Lavazza-branded espresso machines, the large, yellow, and steel, OJ making machines were ubiquitous in cafés along the Camino. Perhaps the same salesperson sold both machines. I confused the barista when I asked if I could have my OJ to go. Years ago, a Spanish friend told me that one way she identified Americans in Spain was by their habit of eating and drinking while walking. "Americans are always in a hurry," she said. So, while it seemed Americans asking for coffee to go was now accepted, asking for OJ to go was still a novel idea. I said just put it in a to-go coffee cup. That solved the issue.

I again took up the middle spot in our group's walk: Adam and Rosemary minutes ahead of me and the Davidsons minutes behind. I had many moments of isolation, lost in my thoughts, but it also gave me the opportunity to speak to more pilgrims.

One woman I met, Evelyn, was dressed in red leggings and a sports top. From Florida, she was walking solo and had started in St. Jean Pied de Port and said it was something she had always wanted to do. I was impressed seeing so many people walking the Camino solo, especially women. According to American Pilgrims on the Camino, in 2022, 231,462 women received their Compostela versus 206,861 men – almost 25,000 more women. Our group was a perfect example of this ratio: four women and three men. Of our travelers, Rosemary and Olivia are the most eager to walk the Camino again and next time from Port Jean de Port.

Rosemary and Adam waited for me at a Roman-built five-arched stone bridge that led into Melide. We were closing in on Santiago, passing our halfway mark today. Perhaps this is why even though today's walk was only 2 km shorter than yesterday's, it seemed a lot quicker. Everyone's demeanor and energy levels were up as we walked into town.

To add to that positive energy, the town of Melide felt confident and self-sufficient. There were more people on the sidewalks, in the restaurants, and in the businesses of which there was a large variety.

Perhaps it was because the town sat at the crossroads where two Camino routes joined: the Camino Primitivo, the oldest Camino route and the one the young lovebirds at the train station in Madrid were walking, and the Camino Francés that we were on.

Or perhaps it was the large variety of people in the town's population. I saw the Galician pale skin and dark features, the bronzed skin of Andalusians, and a mix of blonds and brunettes. A pretty cosmopolitan mix. As if to confirm this fact, there were several female intimate apparel stores here. An odd observation I know, but I never noticed similar female stores in Spain. Another sign of happy people?

The sun broke through the cloud cover just before we went to lunch. We had a beautiful meal at

Casa Alongos which had picnic tables set up under green trees on their large grassy lawn to enjoy the sunshine. The glasses of tinto de verano completed the day's perfect vibe.

On the way back to our albergue, we stopped at Alborada for churros y chocolate. The café had a bar, ice cream counter, and a full kitchen menu. It tried to cover all the food bases. As we ate our churros, Adam spotted an antelope head mounted on a wall. It seemed odd, but then I found another store in Melide that I had not seen anywhere else in Spain, one that sold hunting rifles.

I had thought owning a gun was illegal in Spain, since I rarely heard of gun violence here. I learned citizens and legal residents can own guns in Spain, but there are a lot more regulations than in the U.S. For example, in Spain a buyer must pass a background check, as well as a psychological and medical test every year. In addition, they must pass a practical and theoretical exam. In the state of Kentucky, a gun buyer just needs an ID and to pass an instant background check.

The reason why I was at a store that sold guns was because I was looking for new sunglasses. Back in Toledo, I had stepped on my old ones when I got out of a taxi. In Melide, there were lots of optometrists, but the sunglasses were expensive, from $60 to $200. No cheap $20 knock offs. Fortunately, I found a pair for 39.90 euro at the sporting goods store, Armería Rúa (Armory Street). The sporting goods store was small, the size of a large living room, but it was packed to the ceiling with camping equipment, fishing gear, hiking boots, outdoor clothing, and the aforementioned guns.

The Davidsons also took advantage of Melide's wide variety of shops. We were halfway done with our Camino and their luggage was still chasing them around Spain. With the colder weather, they were done waiting for their clothes to find them.

Locating our albergue, O Candil, was tricky. While it was located on Rúa Principal, the official Camino pathway, the street ran parallel to the town's main street of Avenida de Lugo causing us to initially search the wrong street. Shouldn't a street named Principal Street be the main street? Once we found the right street, we passed the albergue too. Our city navigational abilities must've been getting rusty. Every town after Sarria had been much smaller than Melide. With 7400 people, Melide was twice the size of Palas de Rei, which was twice the size of Portomarín. I imagined we would be completely lost once we arrived in Santiago de Compostela.

Eventually we did find O Candil's bronze plaque on the side of a white building. The plaque told the story of how the building had once been a former brass workshop where lanterns and oil lamps were once manufactured. Hence the albergue's name, O Candil, or The Oil Lamp.

O Candil's immaculate interior matched perfectly with its owner who wore a V-neck sweater, tie, pressed slacks, and polished dress shoes. Like

O Caballo Verde, this was a true albergue: a room with four bunk beds and a communal bathroom. Rosemary had been nervous about this albergue before we arrived. It would be the one time on the trip where it did not meet her requirement of a private bathroom or one we only shared with the Davidsons. Fortunately, she only had to share it with one woman from another family.

I was writing my day's notes at a table in the albergue's communal dining area when the family passed by on their way out to dinner.

"Great, to see fellow Americans," I said. "Where did you start from?"

"We started with our son in Sarria," the woman said. She was in her 30s, wearing light makeup, black yoga pants and light-weight hoodie, and had shoulder length curly black hair. She looked like an upscale yoga member.

"He is not your son," the man said. He was in his early 50s with salt and pepper hair and had a reserved countenance that seemed like he analyzed everything before he spoke. Lawyer perhaps? Those were the only words I heard him speak during our stay.

There was a quick downturn to her smile and a cloud over her features, but then she brightened up. "Right, how silly of me."

The teenager was quiet. Waiting at the door to leave.

She grabbed the man's hand. "Well, we better be going."

Later that evening, the teenager was in the lobby looking at his phone, and I was under the impression the adults were spending some alone time together. I had also seen a young Spanish couple check in, no backpacks and dressed nicely, obviously not pilgrims. I never found bunk beds particularly romantic, but as I learned on this Camino, everyone's intention for being here is different.

Tomorrow: Valleys and Big Paella

DAY 7

Arzúa 14 km

We met the Davidsons in the communal dining area for breakfast. The doors to the other rooms were open and all the other guests were gone even though it was only 8 am. We were definitely not the early birds of the Camino. The owner had fresh bread delivered that morning and he had stocked the refrigerator with fruit and milk, including lactose-free for me. Louie tried to figure out the coffee grinder/maker process but gave up. We knew we would find plenty of places for coffee along the road if precedent continued. After a breakfast of ham, bread, fruit, and Coco Puffs we headed out.

Wow! Today was rain day. The weather switched between heavy drizzle and rain all day. My waterproof gear kept me good and dry. Everyone else wore ponchos and rain jackets, except Adam of course. He still didn't think it was real rain.

He sounded more like someone from rain-soaked Seattle rather than drought-stricken Los Angeles. Fortunately for him, the tape we had put on the inner soles of his wet shoes held, as did the Kompeed and bandages that were on his feet.

My feet and energy felt good. I had settled into a consistent rhythm and pace. Good thing too as this leg was the most physically challenging of our Camino. While it was not the longest, it was the hilliest. Add mud and rain, it was a grind.

At the bottom of one valley, a dozen pilgrims, including two bikers, waited to cross a small stream using a narrow row of rocks. Even though the stream was only six-feet across and two-feet deep in the middle, a pilgrim couldn't walk through it unless they wore waders, otherwise water would get into their boots. Funny how such a small amount of water could be a serious obstacle.

During the day, we walked past many ruins of empty homes and buildings, the most I had seen along the Camino. They were the clearest sign of the depopulating towns of Galicia. Whether it was because of the depopulation or because we were walking deeper into Galicia, further from Madrid, independence graffiti became more prolific: "Free the Patriots," "F* Spain," etc. on walls and under overpasses.

But not all the buildings along this stretch were in ruins. There were still lively albergues and cafes along the way. We stopped at Bar "No Camino" that served decent coffee and good anise cake. Its green

Astroturf outside and red table umbrellas gave it a welcoming Christmas feel.

The number of pilgrims filling the road increased daily, but we still found our friends from Casa Morgade throughout the day. While walking with the couple from Sevilla, Hugo asked me, "Are you Catholic, John?"

"No," I said.

"Excuse me for asking, but then why are you walking?"

"Rosemary always wanted to do this as she is Catholic. I came to support her, and it sounded like a fun adventure."

"But you are not Catholic?"

"No, I am agnostic. I believe in a higher power that created life and listens, but not a formal organized religion."

"I could tell you had religion in your life." He patted my shoulder. "I suspect that subconsciously that is the reason you are doing the Camino."

I was not sure I agreed with him, but while on the Camino, I did give thanks every night before I went to bed to my higher power for giving me the ability physically, mentally, and financially to be here.

Arriving in Arzúa, after a long final uphill walk, we found Jessica and Ray. They stood at the city's information kiosk and were stressed. Their travel agent had booked them at an albergue 8km outside of town and they didn't know it. They had wanted to stay in town and were physically done walking for the day. Fortunately, the woman at the kiosk was able to arrange transportation to the albergue. A few days later, Ray told me that the albergue was set in a beautiful location, but they would have preferred staying in town so they could have explored it.

Ray and Jessica were not the only ones with lodging difficulties. One of the Davidsons had severe pet allergies, and pets were permissible at our albergue, so they stayed in an apartment a half mile away. It was the only time we stayed in different accommodations along the Camino. Not bad considering the limited number of rooms available in each place we stayed and the family's pet restriction.

But they did have some great news waiting for them when they checked in. Air Canada had finally delivered their luggage! Eleven days after their arrival in Spain and seven days into our Camino, Roxanna and Olivia could finally wear their proper Camino clothes.

At our albergue, Albergue Pension Cima do Lugar, we had individual beds, no more bunkbeds for us, a private bathroom making Rosemary happy, and big windows with a nice view of the main street allowing us to watch pilgrims as they walked into town.

I had spotted where to eat as soon as we arrived, much like in Melide. In Melide, I had seen that beautiful grass lawn and patio at Casa Alongos and knew we would eat there. In Arzúa, I saw a large 4-foot-diameter cast iron pan in front of Encontro

Arzúa where they were cooking a huge batch of paella. The scent of saffron and spices wafted out of the restaurant. It reminded me of the time I spent in the small Spanish town of Exfiliana decades ago and watched their cooks prepare paella in an enormous dish for their annual festival. Along with the paella, we ordered fish, and Caldo Gallego. Caldo Gallego is a traditional Galician vegetable stew that this restaurant serves in a tall clay pot. All three were delicious. While Rosemary and I were going full Spanish menu, Adam was delighted that they sold regular spaghetti with meat sauce. "Nothing new or unusual," he said. "Just plain spaghetti. It reminds me of home."

As the Davidsons left for their lodgings, we made plans to meet for breakfast at Café os Casqueiros on the southern corner of Azrúa's small tree-shaded central plaza. We did this using the antiquated method of, "I will meet you here tomorrow at 8 am." I call this method antiquated since my family's phones didn't work, we would be unable to text or call each other if we were late or something happened. It felt so strange in this age of cellphones and computers not to be able to reach someone instantaneously.

There was a brief respite from the rain in the late afternoon, so I walked around town. Even though Azrúa's population was about the same as Melide's it had a smaller commercial area. There were few shops oriented toward tourists. Most catered to locals and there was one with chic men's clothing that had octopi on lots of their shirts. Pulpo Gallego (Galician Octopus) is the regional dish, so I assumed this was the reason for the sea animal on their clothes.

About 10 pm, a large group of high schoolers marched around and through the town, laughing, joking, and singing. They made 3 rounds by our window. Did they do this nightly? My wife said a tradition in Mexico was for people to walk around plazas at night once the weather cooled down, talking, and meeting up. In Mexico, this tradition is called a Paseo. She said this was how her Mom and Dad had met. Wikipedia said Paseos are traditions in both Mexico and Spain, it appeared we had just heard Azrúa's version.

Tomorrow: Teresa's Amazing Food

DAY 8

A Salceda 11 km

The glow of Café os Casqueiros' yellow lights and its hardwood interior looked warm and inviting as we approached through the drizzling morning. Several pilgrims were eating breakfast when we entered, but not the Davidsons. They were late because they didn't know what to wear now that their luggage had arrived. They had so many choices. And they couldn't let us know because...no phone service.

Once they arrived, we ate a hearty American breakfast with toast, eggs, good coffee and the girls ate the local Arzúa-Ulloa cheese. Arzúa is famous for its soft cheese which has a protected designation of origin registration. The designation means only cheese produced from this region's cows can use that name. Unfortunately, I am lactose intolerant, so I was unable to try it, but the girls liked it, remarking on its smooth creamy texture.

Once again everyone spent a lot of time walking solo, alone with their thoughts. We were spread out all along the road. It seemed like the more days we walked, the more we were comfortable with being alone, even savoring those moments. While I enjoyed meeting pilgrims and talking with my family and friends, the conversations did keep me away from my own thoughts. Sometimes I felt like I intruded upon other people's solitude. There was a fine balance to meeting those two desires, but after days of walking I was learning the tells: the inviting smile vs. the avoidance of eye contact, the slowdown to match my speed vs. the walk past without slowing, the quick "Buen Camino" vs. a wave combined with a "Buen Camino", etc.

While Adam still sprinted ahead, blisters and all, the Davidson's were slowing down. I think something caused Louie pain, but he never complained, except about bad coffee, and kept any other negative sentiments close to his fisherman's vest. He carried all kinds of things in its dozen pockets. It was a running joke that he always had what someone needed, although it could take a few moments for him to find it: lip balm, sunscreen, phone, even a roll of toilet paper were all in that vest.

The breakfast and coffee that morning set us up well for the day's walk. We only stopped two times, and neither one was for food or for very long, which made Adam happy.

Ahead of me, pilgrims gazed off the road to the right between a break in a dirt berm that blocked our view of the land beyond. A few stepped off the road and into the gap taking pictures. Intrigued, I followed. A great stand of pine trees covered in green vines that seemed to go on forever lay behind the berm. Their towering, organized rows looked like dark tunnels leading to a mystical land of faeries and dark spirits. Were the trees planted for wood harvesting? If so, the dense vines would make the job difficult. Perhaps we were passing a magical forest after all.

Magic on my mind, I came upon a bar covered in brown beer bottles-Tia Dolores. Thousands of bottles hung upside down throughout the small building and large patio, over its entrance, along its walls and fences, and in tree stumps. Messages of love, wishes, desires, jokes, and names, were written with white pen on them. Humans want to leave a mark. Be remembered. I wanted to leave my mark too, but didn't want to down a beer before I finished today's journey, so I asked if I could buy an empty beer bottle. The employee squinted at me not understanding. I am surprised no one has ever asked her this before and asked again. She said no. Perhaps I am strange. I left, leaving no mark here, except for the laugh she will undoubtedly have with her coworkers about the American who wanted to buy an empty beer bottle. Or maybe I spawned a new business idea in her mind. Collect nearby bars' empty beer bottles and sell them to the occasional strange pilgrim. I smiled.

Outside, Rosemary petted a calico-patterned cat.

I knew I married a cat lady but didn't realize I was surrounded by them. Rosemary, Roxanna, and the girls would stop and say hi or try to pet every cat they saw. How different men and women are, at least the ones in our group. We, the men, could care less if there was a domestic house pet and just walked on. However, when I saw big woolly sheep in an expansive green field, I stopped and admired them. Horses, or bulls, or cows, or goats...things I could not see back in Los Angeles would get me to stop and watch.

Our walk was short today and like our last short walk, Adam bypassed our albergue. Fortunately, this time he was only a couple hundred feet ahead of me, so when he looked back and saw me crossing the highway to Casa Tia Teresa, he hurried back.

"Coffee now?" he said, annoyed.

"No, this is our albergue for tonight."

His frown turned into a big smile.

We waited for the others on Casa Tia Teresa's covered patio, I was in the lead with Adam for once. We had a splendid view of the highway where we watched pilgrims walking uphill in the rain, past us, toward A Salceda. On our albergue's wooden fence stood a few beer bottles, obviously, mimicking Tia Dolores' bottle gimmick.

We entered and saw a young man at the bar writing in a large paperbound ledger book and ubiquitous OJ and Lavazza espresso machines behind him on the counter. Alejandro was the receptionist, waiter, busser, bartender, pretty much every job who was not a cook or housekeeping.

Checking in, Adam scored because he had his own room again. Both of our rooms were large enough to accommodate three people, ours even had three beds, but Booking.com said the albergue had a two person per room maximum occupancy. We savored the luxury of the extra space, privacy, and our own bathroom. As good as our accommodation was, the most amazing thing about Casa Tia Teresa was its food.

I started lunch with an Irish hot chocolate, hot chocolate with Baileys, to remove the chill from today's cold rain and then asked Alejandro for a lunch suggestion. He said the bocadillo de chicharrons was really good.

I am from Southern California and love Mexican food, so I thought I knew what chicharrons were: deep fried pig skin. I never heard of them being placed on a sandwich. Alejandro saw my face of disapproval and said, "Trust me, it is very good. They are Galician Chicharrons. We cook them on the grill, not fried. And they are not fatty. Very tender."

Who was I to disagree with our host, so I placed my order.

What he served looked more like carnitas on a baguette. There was not a globule of pork fat or grease anywhere. Alejandro said Casa Tia Teresa renders the fat from the belly meat leaving their chicharrons lean, tender, and flavorful.

As soon as Louie tried mine, he ordered it as well. Rosemary and Roxanna ordered Irish hot chocolates too. I love being a trendsetter!

Like Casa Morgade and Casa Perdigueira, Casa Tia Teresa was isolated, meaning peace and quiet. Since there was nowhere to go after lunch, we relaxed in our rooms or the lobby. The albergue also offered laundry services which Rosemary and the Davidson's took advantage of. I handwashed my own clothes of course. By now, I was a handwashing pro.

After a shower, I really got into the mood and sang along to some Blink 182 songs on my phone. When I looked out the second-floor window, I saw a couple of preteens sitting below. Ha! I hoped they liked my singing. Maybe I became a meme in the Twitter-verse.

In the late afternoon, I went down to the lobby for a snack. As I stepped into the lobby, the smell of roasted garlic and spices washed over me. The restaurant's two cooks in white aprons prepared to dig into their late lunch. On each of their plates was a big fold of meat, like a tent, sitting atop french fries covered in a brown broth. It smelled amazing.

"Perdón, señora, qué comes? It smells so good," I said. (Excuse me, what are you eating.)

With a crooked smile the shorter one said, "Oreja de cerdo y chorizo." (Pig ear and chorizo.)

Like the chicharrons, my preconceived notions about food were being challenged here. It smelled so good; I was excited for dinner.

Alejandro ran the whole dinner as waiter, barista, and busser.

We started with the pimientos de padrón, croquetas de jamón, and tinto de verano. All most excellent.

The Caldo Gallego here, unlike in Arzúa, had little pieces of pork. I was never told what part of the pig the meat came from, but considering I had seen ear served, and ate chicharrons already, it was probably better not to know.

When I asked Alejandro what he recommended for dinner, he said, "the Lomo especial Casa Tia Teresa," and smiled. “It is very good. I recommend it.” Since his previous recommendation panned out, I said, “Sure, let’s go for it.” I mean it couldn’t be any stranger than pig ear or mystery stew meat, right?

It was pig knuckle.

Yes, pig knuckle. I didn’t even know pigs had knuckles. It was served as a rectangular piece of meat, about four inches high, three inches wide, and four inches long, covered in a red sauce that smelled warm and peppery. As I stuck my fork and knife in, they sunk into a thick layer of fat. I guess I was going to eat pork fat after all. Disappointing. Then I looked at a diner at a table next to me who had ordered the same thing. I guess he had eaten pig knuckle before. He just slid off that top 2-inches of fat to reach the meat below. That was half my main course. But when in Spain do as the Spaniards, right?

Oh, my goodness! I must say, those two inches of meat below were some of the most savory and juiciest pork I had ever eaten. Alejandro came through again.

Roxanna had the lubina (European sea bass) and she loved it. It would be her favorite meal of the trip. Louie also enjoyed his large steak.

The only drawback was the menu was very meat heavy, so the vegetarians were stuck with cheese sandwiches and veggie scrambles. The girls did score with their dessert: musse de queso y membrillo (muss cheese and quince jam). The cheese was a famous soft cheese for the region and the sweet red jam set off the creamy cheese perfectly. The rest of us ate pineapple cake and tarta de Santiago for dessert. The Casa Tia Teresa dinner was a true epicurean feast.

Bellies stuffed, we were ready to tackle what was scheduled to be our longest walk of the Camino the next day.

Tomorrow: Pizza Delivery

DAY 9

San Paio 15 km

Crowing roosters and chirping birds woke me before my alarm. Early morning fog lay across the farmland. A clear shadow-blue sky marked the end of rain for the remainder of our Camino.

Rosemary slept while I performed my daily Nike workout and watched the hazy orange sun creep over the horizon. The workout was needed after last night's heavy dinner. I looked forward to our longest walk of the Camino. Not just for burning off the extra calories, but the challenge of it. It was our longest planned walk, 15km. I had the same excitement that I felt before I descended a particularly challenging slope while snowboarding. I would tighten my gloves, acknowledge my abilities, visualize my path, and with mind focused, set off.

Today was our eighth day of walking and I had

my routine down. I checked my pack: rain gear, snacks, water, and first aid kit. I inspected my toes, replacing two out of nine old Kompeed patches. I had removed my extra shoe inserts and now only wore one layer of socks since the Kompeed patches covered my hotspots, thereby relieving the tightness in the shoe box around my toes. My feet were holding up well.

However, Adam's feet were in bad shape. His blisters were really bothering him. He said he had been walking on his toes to keep pressure off his right heel, thereby creating a new blister on the bottom of that foot. No wonder he wanted to complete our daily walks quick. The quicker the walk, the less time on his feet. I spent a few minutes inspecting them, ignoring his multiple, "It's fine, Dad, don't worry about it." Then I replaced the lamb's wool, added more, affixed additional Kompeed patches, and checked for folds in his inner sole. I must've done a great job, as he was flying today.

After breakfast, only OJ and toast for me after last night's feast, our group departed together, but soon separated: Adam and Rosemary upfront, the Davidson's behind, and me somewhere in the middle. Unlike yesterday where I could see everyone, as if connected by an invisible thread, today we were disconnected, free flowing, each on their own independent journey, yet still attached by the Camino. A Camino that I knew would eventually lead me back to my companions.

I will admit, today's particularly wide gaps between us were primarily my fault. I had stopped at the Mesón A'Esquipa café for my daily café con leche, but no one else did. Not even Louie who always stopped for a caffeine hit. Still, I thought I would quickly catch up to the slower-paced Davidson's. It baffled me as each hour passed that I did not. Lack of a cellphone was haunting me again.

Stepping out of Mesón A'Esquipa, I was happily surprised to see Ray and Jessica sitting at a white plastic table, napkins and forks set in front of them. Ray waved me over. "I read they serve one of the best tortilla españolas in Spain here," he said. "We had to stop."

Jessica just smiled, accustomed to Ray's enthusiasm to try everything on the Camino.

"You should join us," he said.

I almost did. I mean how could I not try one of the best tortillas in Spain?

"That sounds really tempting," I said, "but I have to catch up with my group."

I looked back at the two of them waiting alone under the trees as I started down the road and felt a twinge of guilt at not sharing in their experience and comradeship.

Ray and Jessica found me on the trail a couple of hours later and said that while the tortilla española was good, they couldn't say it was the best they had ever had. That news told me that I had made the right choice to chase after my group. And yes, I was walking so slow that an 80-year-old man had a sit-down meal and still caught up and passed me.

Further along the Camino, a middle-aged man with long flowing blond hair, dressed in black was passing by me, but then slowed for a quick chat. Andre was from Germany and said, "I started the Camino to quit smoking. Two months ago, I woke up and could barely breathe and knew I had to stop. So, I booked a flight, and started walking three weeks ago. I had been smoking a pack a day since I was 20 and have not lit one since."

I was impressed by his quicker pace as I had never smoked, and he was raring to pull ahead.

"I hate walking," he said. "I just want to get this done."

"So, you wouldn't come back?"

"Only if I start smoking again, and I don't want to start smoking again."

Before he left me in his dust, he told me that he had started walking in St. Jean Pied de Port and then took a bus through the Meseta to Leon to cut off a few weeks from his walk because he had to get back to work.

The Meseta is a 200-kilometer plain between Burgos and León, sparsely populated, and with little shade. The landscape is quite different from the green trees and grass of Galicia. Crossing the Meseta by public transportation like Andre was not uncommon. This is the same stretch where the female Instagrammer I had mentioned earlier had done the same thing. However, most pilgrims I spoke to who started in St. Jean Pied de Port walked the full Camino Francés enjoying the variety of landscapes.

Tamara told me she walked across the Meseta during the heat wave. The young woman, from Slovakia with her blond hair in a bun and dressed all in red, she had started her Camino seven weeks ago as a challenge to herself and saw the heated Meseta as just another obstacle to overcome. Her journey, like Andre's, was a solo one. But unlike Andre's she was taking her time, resting often, including spending multiple nights in Pamplona, Burgos, and León. Today was the exception to her leisurely pace. "Today, I am walking 30 kilometers," she said.

"Why the hurry?"

"Because my flight is tomorrow morning."

"How is your body holding up?"

"It has been great until today?"

"What's wrong?"

"I tweaked my knee." She laughed. "Today of all days, right?"

Then she left me in her dust too, walking with a barely perceptible limp.

Yes, more people were passing me on the Camino, than I was passing them.

Ray, Andre, and Tamara's interactions today reinforced my belief that everyone's Camino was unique. Intentions, pace, and even clothing were all different, yet all right in their own way. Why was Andre wearing all black non-hiking garb? Why was Tamara wearing all red? Why on this day, were the Davidson girls still wearing Rosemary's clothes when they now had their own? If I can retain this openness and understanding towards others when I return home, I know my life will be happier and fuller.

I caught up with Rosemary and Adam at the 15k Bar two hours later. They were finishing a chocolate croissant.

"OK, Mom we can go now," Adam said.

"I need to take a break," I said.

Adam rolled his eyes as I sat down and put my feet up on a chair.

"How long?" he said, backpack on.

"I am going to buy a snack."

"I am going to go, okay?"

"If you want to."

When I came out of 15k with a piece of neon orange carrot cake, they were gone.

I was tired. I had been hurrying without stopping trying to catch someone in my group. Really, I was. I had been worried someone may have gotten lost or hurt as I hadn't seen any of them in so long. The cake gave me a nice sugar boost and after resting 10 minutes I was ready to go for the final leg.

And who did I happen to see walking up the road as I put my backpack on? The Davidsons. The only pilgrims in Spain who did not pass me it would seem. I missed them because they had turned onto a side trail through a nearby village a few miles back. I was relieved. No one was lost. My group's invisible threads had been reconnected. I headed after Rosemary and Adam as the Davidson's settled in for their break.

From the 15k Bar onward, I felt that I had arrived back in civilization. There were still trees, farmland, and pilgrims, but there were subtle and not so subtle changes that we were nearing a big city. For example, the 15k Bar sat on the corner of two principal roads with no homes nor lodging nearby. The employees had to commute to get here. I also passed a huge recreation center filled with families and had to walk around an airport. Santiago de Compostela felt so close now.

I arrived in San Paio at 1:15 pm, only four hours and fifteen minutes after I had left Casa Tia Teresa. Unlike the Castromaior to Palas de Rei hike, we knew today was a long walk, so we minimized our stops. Our only significant stop was the 15k Bar...and mine at Meson A'Esquipa.

Adam and Rosemary were sitting at the Casa Porta bodega at the entrance to the town, waiting for me, not realizing that our stop for the night was only 50 yards down the road. The Davidson's soon arrived, and we headed to our final albergue of the Camino, The Last 12k.

The Last 12k was a cute stone-walled albergue with a sharp-elbowed owner who ran the kitchen and front desk. Her husband cleaned and prepared the rooms. They were in their 60s and one young female cook helped in the kitchen. Our room was spotless, with a view of the local church across the street, and the pillows were embroidered with L12k.

We were all famished and ate at Casa Porta

where I had first met Adam and Rosemary. For lunch, Adam ate spaghetti, and the girls ate salads that to their delight included watermelon chunks. The adults ordered shared plates: Roxanna's favorite padrón peppers, a ham and parmesan cheese plate, a fish dish, and Louie's Camino go-to: ham and cheese croquettes. Delicious chocolate cake finished off our meal.

One important note about this town, everything closes at 4 pm. Everything being the bodega and the albergue. Rosemary wondered if there was a vampire problem with the whole shut down before dark vibe. The small old church that sat just outside our window and the town's stone buildings added to the creepy effect.

If everything closes at 4pm, what does a pilgrim do for dinner? The albergue owner had a menu from a pizza place from the "next" town over. Pizza delivery on the Camino? Sure, why not? We ordered a margarita, a vegetarian, and a Hawaiian pizza as well as a tropical salad and ate them on the church steps. They hit the spot, especially with the vegetarians.

The air was chilly and the sun still shining as I took the empty boxes to the town's dumpsters around 8 pm. Two kids played in a creek trying to catch tadpoles with their grandma watching nearby. I wondered what it would be like growing up here. There were less than 100 people in town, meaning there were few kids to play with, and then there were all these strangers, speaking a multitude of languages, walking through in outlandish garb.

In comparison, I was born in a city of four million people, Los Angeles. My high school had 2,000 students. While there were exponentially a lot more people, Los Angeles was still a community. It was a melting pot of immigrants from Korea, Mexico, Armenia, and dozens of other countries rivaling the number of countries Camino pilgrims originated from, yet they lived, worked, and went to school there. They were part of its community, dwarfing the number of transitory tourists. In Sao Paio, the pilgrims just passed through, not settling down, not establishing roots. They were like fallen leaves catching a breeze and blowing through, most never stopping, a few for a quick lunch, and even fewer overnight.

We were asleep before nightfall and any vampires descended upon the town.

Tomorrow: What Is Most Important

DAY 10

Santiago de Compostela
12 km

This is it! Our final day of walking and no vampire bites on our neck.

Downstairs, pilgrims ate breakfast, smiled and spoke loud and fast. Pilgrims passing by our albergue had an extra pep in their step. Journeys were coming to an end.

After a full breakfast of eggs, toast, OJ, and coffee, we were off. As if that wasn't enough food, on the outskirts of Lavacolla a half hour later, a couple sold homemade powdered donuts. Their primary customers were locals leaving the nearby Cathedral of San Paio Da Sabugueira. "Do as the locals do," is my motto, so I bought a bag. I told the lady I only wanted a half bag, so I don't get fat. Her large husband smiled and said, "What are you trying to say?"

A little further on, the cat ladies found a pure white cat intertwined atop a green gate and spent a good five minutes oohing and ahhing over it. Adam shook his head and limped off down the road. I shook my head too, but being the dutiful husband, I waited with Louie until the ladies were done.

As we walked with the sun behind us, I made shadow puppets on the road. To my surprise, Ray and Jessica ran up and asked me what I was doing. Yes, ran. We all started laughing as I said I just wanted to play.

At Restaurante Cafetería A Calzada, I had my last Lavazza latte of the Camino, then continued and crested Monte do Gozo (Mountain of Joy). And here, I saw, the city of Santiago de Compostela spread out before me, less than 5 kilometers away. Even better, I saw the Cathedral de Santiago with its twin bell towers rising through the cityscape of 100,000 people. The mountain's name was appropriate.

Rosemary and I walked together the rest of the way. It was the longest just the two of us had walked together on the Camino. I enjoyed sharing this last part with her, my inspiration for the trip. She was beaming as we reached the red-lettered entrance sign to the city and stopped to wait for the Davidsons.

While we waited, Ray and Jessica caught up again. We agreed that running into each other's families throughout the journey was one of our trip's highlights. Our random meetings connected me in a personal way with the Camino. More grounded. Like when you leave your house and see your good neighbors day in and day out or run into a friend at the grocery store. Unfortunately, we didn't see Ray and Jessica again.

Then three Spanish high school groups passed us, indicating just how many students walk the Camino. I imagined that a trip like this brought history to life for them, instilled pride in their country, and tightened their societal bonds. We spoke to two chaperones who waited for their students to arrive.

"Most of the chaperones take the school bus from place to place," the older balding man said. "We handle the more challenging tasks of night monitors, managing money, and getting the students settled in."

"Walking is the easy part," his younger full bearded partner continued. "Those chaperones only have to be available for emergencies and to catch stragglers."

I am sure the chaperones who walked in the heat and rain may have had a different opinion of which chaperones' jobs were more challenging.

Once the Davidsons made it to the sign, we headed out. Veronica and Roxanna stayed with us awhile then fell back to be with Olivia and Louie. Rosemary and I continued on, holding hands. Cafes and stores lined the cobblestone streets trying to get our attention, but there was no stopping us. The end was so close, I could feel it. During the last 30 minutes, I kept expecting to see the tunnel to Plaza del Obradoiro and the Cathedral around the next corner of whitewashed buildings.

I heard the entrance before I saw it: the unique melodic high whine of bagpipe music floating through the sunlit air. There were no castanets here. This was Galicia, the land of Celtic influence.

The music pulled me in, into the downward sloping tunnel, under arches supporting a six-story gothic building, past the bagpiper, and out into the sweeping Plaza del Obradoiro.

But what I focused on as we exited the tunnel was my son. Not a building, not the physical destination, but Adam limping over to us with a huge smile, proudly proclaiming that he had finished 40 minutes ago. That joy in his face and our subsequent family hug at the end of our journey emphasized what was most important to me.

Releasing my family, I took in my impressive surroundings.

The Cathedral de Santiago dominated the Eastern side of the plaza. Its soaring twin bell towers and 230-foot-wide Baroque façade adorned with Saints and pillars made for a fitting end to a 10- or 40-day journey. It was like finding the X on a treasure map. Pilgrims took pictures in front of its wrought iron black gates, others lost in thought sat or laid out on the plaza stones taking in its magnificence, and others laughed and talked in small or large groups. New arrivals, like us, wore backpacks, but many had none, indicating they had already checked into their albergues.

To the North sat the broad four-story Hostal dos Reis Católicos completed in 1511 by Queen Isabella to serve as the Royal Hospital to care for pilgrims at the end of their journey. It served as a hospital for four centuries, but is now a five-star hotel, the Parador de Santiago de Compostela. I checked the prices in March 2023 for June 1, 2023, and a double standard room with the special pilgrim's discount and breakfast cost 319.60 euro.

To the West sat the newest building on the plaza, the Neoclassical Pazo de Raxoi, built in 1766. It had more windows than the other buildings surrounding the plaza, perhaps due to architectural improvements over the centuries. Its broad rectangular shape complemented the towering vertical cathedral across from it.

To the South was the relatively smaller Colexio de San Xerome with a single bell tower founded in 1501. But the building I was happiest to see to the South was our hotel for the night, the white-washed Apartamentos Inferniños right next to the college. There would be no wandering around looking for our hotel today. It was right there!

Two minutes later, the Davidsons arrived. After pictures, hearty congratulations, and soaking in the views, we went to our respective lodgings. Our host, Ana, reminded me of Snow White with her snow-white skin, rosy cheeks, and jet-black hair. She said Galicians love the sun but burn very easily since they see so little of it.

According to Booking.com, the building that

was now Apartamentos Inferniños was built in 1666 and sits on a street that once led from the Cathedral to the less pious areas of town. The view from our room of the plaza and cathedral was priceless. Even though the building was over 300 years old, our room had all the modern amenities: full kitchen, personal washer and dryer, and private bathroom. The only ancient looking items in the apartment were the dark wood floors. Be careful of splinters.

For dinner, we met the Davidsons at El Marte, a restaurant specializing in tortilla españolas. El Marte's tortilla españolas served as a base, like the crust on a pizza, then they were topped with various ingredients. Ours was topped with sauced lomo (pork) and the vegetarians had a salad on theirs. It was a lot of food as customers were served an entire tortilla española, not just a slice. One could easily feed three people.

Afterwards, Rosemary and I visited the Cathedral de Santiago while everyone else went to their rooms. There was no line. A visitor only had to wait if they were attending mass. We entered through the Puerta de las Platerías (Door of the Silversmiths) in the cross's southern arm. The interior of the Cathedral was laid out like a cross. Two rows of stone pillars stretched across the Cathedral. In the center, hanging above the central dais, was the largest censer in the world, the botafumeiro. During mass, the 180-pound silver censer would swing over the congregants through a system of thick chains and pulleys spreading smoke from its burning incense.

A solid silver altar and gilded choir stalls stood at the head of the cross. Four angels held a large golden canopy above the altar where St. James was seated. Everything except the skin of the angels and saints was covered in gold and silver. While the space was stunning, it did display the dichotomy between the wealth of the Catholic Church and the poverty of so many of its congregants throughout the centuries and even today. Another interesting feature of the altar was the prominence of St. James and the absence of Jesus. Catholic churches in the United States almost always have Jesus as the central focal point and usually hanging on a cross.

From the shiny and bright, we descended a narrow staircase beneath the altar to view the dim crypt. It was eerie. Here lay the relics of Saint James and two of his disciples. In the Catholic faith, relics refer to a Saint's physical remains like bones and teeth. They could be displayed in a vessel, like the silver urn here, or exposed for viewing like they are in Sevilla's grand cathedral. Creepy.

Having reached our final religious destination, it was now time to officially complete our Camino. We picked up Adam and walked to the Oficina de Acogida al Peregrinos to turn in our Credencials del Peregrino and obtain our Compostelas. At the office, we had to take numbers and complete a survey before we could see a clerk. I was pilgrim number 998 that day. Rosemary received the cool number 1000. The survey asks where you are from, where did you start from, method of transportation, and the reason for walking the Camino. The last question had three choices: religious, non-religious, or both.

Rosemary chose both. While her reasoning was primarily religious, it was also a vacation to spend time with friends and family. Then I saw Adam circle both.

"Why are you circling both?" I asked him.

"The Camino is a religious walk for Catholics," he said.

"I know, but I thought you were walking because you were with your Mom and Dad, not because it was religious."

"I am Catholic, Dad. That's why I came."

It is difficult to get him to church on Sundays except for the obligatory holidays, and he had made no comment during all this time that religion was on his mind, so his response surprised me. After a moment, he did add, "And you and mom made me."

And me?

My original reason was to complete an awesome adventure, to challenge myself, and experience a historic activity. However, as I walked and talked to my fellow pilgrims, I became more aware of and grateful for all the choices, opportunities, and life experiences that have led me to this point in my life; in being able to be here at this moment walking the Camino and writing about it. Was there a higher power guiding my life choices to arrive here? Or did a higher power provide the spark of life to the universe and everything since has been the result of innumerable butterfly effects that I had minimal control over? Or was my thought process created by a mix of atoms, life experiences, and conscious life choices that together brought me to this point? I believe it is a combination of all three. If I believe this, then how can I say my reason for walking the Camino was purely non-religious? Hugo was right after all.

According to the Oficina, in 2019, 40% completed the walk for purely religious reasons, 11% non-religious, and 49% a combination of the two. Even though walking the Camino de Santiago has been a religious tradition for over 1,000 years, perhaps being an American, I was surprised that 89% of pilgrims had at least some religious reason for walking. Perhaps, more people than I imagine have the same existential questions and thoughts that I do concerning religion.

We also paid the extra three euros for the Certificate of Distance that showed our name in Latin, our starting point, Sarria, and 115 km written on it.

Adding to my souvenir collection, at Nova Souvenir across the street, I bought a postcard created by Instagrammer dohwa.ceramic from South Korea. She has walked the entire Camino and parts of it five times and sells her art online and in stores along the Camino. The postcard depicted several tiny pilgrims around a big bowl of pulpo gallego. I felt good supporting a fellow pilgrim in her creativity and business, and in a way thanking her for all the information she had shared about the Camino.

As the sun lowered in the West, we continued our walk around the old city. We passed through the main plaza tunnel again where a young man now sang the overture to The Marriage of Figaro, one of my favorites, had some churros y chocolate at a café behind the Cathedral, and then found the Davidsons at Bar Charra for beers and tinto de veranos to reminisce about our journey.

With the purpling of night, everyone else turned in, but I wandered the streets, not wanting this perfect day to end. The glow of yellow streetlights lit the old buildings, casting shadows down ancient alleyways and across cobblestones. A Meringue-sounding band, guitars, flute, tambourine, and drum, played on a side street with a lively crowd dancing to the tunes. Me too. It's eight members wore black renaissance style pants and tops with purple sashes looped across their chests.

As I returned to the Plaza del Obradoiro, I heard another Galician band playing under the arches of Pazo de Raxoi. They all wore capes, had red sashes, and played stringed instruments with one using a tambourine. As I listened, I looked back across the empty plaza at the illuminated Cathedral set against the starry sky. The Cathedral's interior lights reflected upon its Saints' stone faces. A magical midnight ending to a great journey.

Thank you.

EPILOGUE

We spent two nights in Santiago, then my family rented a car and did a three-night road trip that included Finisterre (the Roman end of the world), the old town of Caceres, and finally Seville. The Davidson's flew to Granada and we all reunited in Hugo's magnificent city for one last Spanish adventure together.

I'd like to thank the amazing people of Spain for providing us with an unforgettable experience.

Living my motto of, "Do it today, tomorrow waits for no one," Rosemary and I plan to walk the Portuguese Way in 2024.

Whatever road, pilgrimage, or adventure you are on in life, I wish you a "Buen Camino."

BIBLIOGRAPHY

Starkie, William. *The Road to Santiago: Pilgrims of St. James*. 1965 ed., Berkeley, University of California Press, 1957.

"Oficina De Acogida Al Peregrino." oficinadelperegrino.com/, 4 Jul. 2023, https://oficinadelperegrino.com/.

"How Spain's Plant-based Dairy Market Is Expanding – Deep Dive, Part One." Just-Food.Com, 24 Jul. 2019, www.just-food.com/features/how-spains-plant-based-dairy-market-is-expanding-deep-dive-part-one/. Accessed 4 Jul. 2023.

"City Population: Palas De Rei." City Population, 1 Jan. 2021,www.citypopulation.de/en/spain/galicia/lugo/27040__palas_de_rei/. Accessed 4 Jul. 2023.

"Camino Statistics." American Pilgrims on the Camino, 23 Apr. 2019, https://americanpilgrims.org/statistics/. Accessed 4 Jul. 2023.

"Rob's Camino." YouTube, uploaded by robscamino, 6 May 2020, www.youtube.com/

watch?v=y9gVRUMdn-A.

"5 Best Tortillas in Madrid." YouTube, uploaded by Spain Revealed, 19 May 2019, www.youtube.com/watch?v=sjL07QFgSwk.

BOOKS BY THIS AUTHOR

Yellowstone And Mt. Rushmore: A Three-Week Road Trip

A man's desire to relive the station wagon road trips of his youth, leads him and his family on a 4013-mile epic journey from the shores of California to the lights of Las Vegas, the geysers of Yellowstone, the granite faces of Mount Rushmore, and one of the largest water parks in the West-Water World. While there are similarities to "National Lampoon's Vacation," John can assure you that no one was tied to the roof.

From Lions To Pharaohs: Book 1 Kenya

Come along as John and his wife visit Kenya's traditional villages, scenic national parks, and photo hunt the Big Five. For ten days, they explore the beautiful country while their jack-of-all trades driver and tour guide tells them stories about the country's complex history and cultures. During the trip, they deal with John's bug phobia, eat meals in the company of a variety of critters, and John is finally able to prove to everyone that the rope he carries with him on every trip really is useful.

10 Days In Egypt: From Lions To Pharaohs Book 2

Riding camels in Egypt, descending into tombs in the Valley of the Kings, and having run-ins with the locals and police...it's all here! Follow John and his wife on their 10-day journey exploring the exotic sun-soaked land from the temple of Abu Simbel in southern Egypt to the romantic city of Alexandria on the Mediterranean coast and everywhere in between. His wife said, "We don't know when we will have this opportunity to visit Egypt again," so they did it all.

www.ingramcontent.com/pod-product-compliance
Lightning Source LLC
Chambersburg PA
CBHW071612040426
42452CB00008B/1327
* 9 7 8 1 7 3 2 8 9 8 4 5 5 *